SAN YUAN
DRAGON GATE
EIGHT FORMATIONS
WATER METHOD

San Yuan Dragon Gate
Eight Formations Water Method

The author can be reached at:

Mastery Academy of Chinese Metaphysics Sdn. Bhd. (611143-A)
19-3, The Boulevard, Mid Valley City,
59200 Kuala Lumpur, Malaysia.
Tel   : +603-2284 8080
Fax   : +603-2284 1218
Email   : info@masteryacademy.com
Website : www.masteryacademy.com

DISCLAIMER:

Published by JY Books Sdn. Bhd. (659134-T)

INDEX

About The Chinese Metaphysics Reference Series

Reference Series

The Chinese Metaphysics Reference Series of books are designed primarily to be used as complimentary textbooks for scholars, students, researchers, teachers and practitioners of Chinese Metaphysics.

The goal is to provide quick easy reference tables, diagrams and charts, facilitating the study and practice of various Chinese Metaphysics subjects including Feng Shui, BaZi, Yi Jing, Zi Wei, Liu Ren, Ze Ri, Ta Yi, Qi Men and Mian Xiang.

This series of books are intended as reference text and educational materials principally for the academic syllabuses of the **Mastery Academy of Chinese Metaphysics**. The contents have also been formatted so that Feng Shui Masters and other teachers of Chinese Metaphysics will always have a definitive source of reference at hand, when teaching or applying their art.

Because each school of Chinese Metaphysics is different, the Reference Series of books usually do not contain any specific commentaries, application methods or explanations on the theory behind the formulas presented in its contents. This is to ensure that the contents can be used freely and independently by all Feng Shui Masters and teachers of Chinese Metaphysics without conflict.

If you would like to study or learn the applications of any of the formulas presented in the Reference Series of books, we recommend that you undertake the courses offered by Joey Yap and his team of Instructors at the Mastery Academy of Chinese Metaphysics.

Other titles offers in the Reference Series:

1. The Chinese Metaphysics Compendium
2. Dong Gong Date Selection
3. Earth Study Discern Truth
4. Xuan Kong Da Gua Structure Reference Book
5. Xuan Kong Da Gua 64 Gua Transformation Analysis
6. Xuan Kong Da Gua Ten Thousand Year Calendar
7. Plum Blossom Divination Book Reference Book
8. BaZi Structures & Structural Useful Gods Reference Book - Wood Structures
9. BaZi Structures & Structural Useful Gods Reference Book - Fire Structures
10. BaZi Structures & Structural Useful Gods Reference Book - Earth Structures
11. BaZi Structures & Structural Useful Gods Reference Book - Metal Structures
12. BaZi Structures & Structural Useful Gods Reference Book - Water Structures
13. The Date Selection Compendium - The 60 Jia Zi Attributes
14. Xuan Kong Purple White Script

Preface

Water plays a fundamental role in Feng Shui – and indeed, it appears that any enthusiast of Feng Shui, whether beginner or professional, is aware of its significance. The reason for its importance is that, in essence, Water acts as a vessel for Qi. Because of its fast-moving, 'Yang' nature, Water can transport or direct Qi toward a particular area, for a particular purpose. But the common problem today is that many people labour under the misconception that any sort of Water formula or method will be able to help them – primarily when it comes to money matters and wealth issues – and as a result, don't pay enough attention to its negative capabilities. Precisely because of its potency, Water also possesses certain negative effects and if used incorrectly or channelled improperly, can cause many catastrophic and ruinous outcomes Water Feng Shui, when applied correctly, can help direct good Qi into and excrete bad Qi from the property.

So it's very important that if one were to use a Water method or formula, one would use the correct kind, and in its proper context. This book talks about a particular system derived from the San Yuan school of Feng Shui – the San Yuan Dragon Gate Eight Formations Water Method. There are various Water methods even under the San Yuan system alone, just as there are many kinds of schools in Feng Shui. But the most popular system under the San Yuan school comes from the Qian Kun Guo Bao 乾坤國寶 (which means Heaven and Earth National Treasure), a classic text supposedly written by Grandmaster Yang Yun Song which encompasses these Dragon Gate Eight Formation Water methods.

Today, the San Yuan Dragon Gate Eight Formations Water Method system is widely practiced all over the world, especially in Hong Kong and Taiwan. It is definitely not the foremost system of water methods, but it is one of the more commonly acceptable ones because of the amount of positive results it has managed to bring about. These positive outcomes along with it's simple calculation have helped cement it as one of the more popular and widely used systems.

As its title suggests, there are Eight Formations used in this system, but within the Eight Formations there are many more transformations within. This book is an attempt to illustrate the various transformations so that it can aid students and practitioners in their attempts to apply the methods to best effect. Although it was primarily designed to help students in the Mastery Academy's Feng Shui Mastery Series as a form of reference and study tool, teachers and students of any school also can use it as an easy reference of research material.

The book has been kept simple – there are only charts and structures available inside, with simple accompanying interpretations or analyses. I've also strived to retain most of the original technical terms and kept the formulas in their original form. This is precisely to enable the use of the book by students and practitioners of any school without conflict in modes or philosophies of teaching. Each teacher will have his or her own interpretation of a formula or method – it's not the case that we all often agree on those key issues. To that end, then, this book should be used under the guidance of a qualified teacher or mentor, who will help the beginner student make sense of the myriad charts and structures and allow you to effectively and correctly apply it for the best possible results. In addition, there is also the option of joining the Mastery Academy's Feng Shui Mastery Series to learn more.

As a final note, please don't let some of the texts and description of water formations in the book scare you. Although some may sound rather "gloomy" or even "detrimental", bear in mind that this is the way ancient texts were written. As this is a transliteration, I did not filter the 'scary' words. In most cases, they may not be so drastic in reality. Also, don't let my earlier warnings about Water methods scare you off from using it, but let it merely serve as a cautionary guideline against adopting a freewheeling and careless style when it comes to Feng Shui methods and applications. Used properly and correctly, these methods can have genuinely transformative results.

I hope that you are able to derive much knowledge and pleasure from using this book. In addition, I wish you best of luck in your quest for more knowledge, and success in your Feng Shui studies and practice.

Joey Yap
September 2010

Author's personal website :
www.joeyyap.com

Academy websites :
www.masteryacademy.com l www.maelearning.com l www.baziprofiling.com

Joey Yap on Facebook :
www.facebook.com/joeyyapFB

MASTERY ACADEMY
OF CHINESE METAPHYSICS™

At **www.masteryacademy.com**, you will find some useful tools to ascertain key information about the Feng Shui of a property or for the study of Astrology.

The Joey Yap Flying Stars Calculator can be utilised to plot your home or office Flying Stars chart. To find out your personal best directions, use the 8 Mansions Calculator. To learn more about your personal Destiny, you can use the Joey Yap BaZi Ming Pan Calculator to plot your Four Pillars of Destiny – you just need to have your date of birth (day, month, year) and time of birth.

For more information about BaZi, Xuan Kong or Flying Star Feng Shui, or if you wish to learn more about these subjects with Joey Yap, logon to the Mastery Academy of Chinese Metaphysics website at **www.masteryacademy.com.**

MASTERY ACADEMY
E-LEARNING CENTER
www.maelearning.com

www.maelearning.com

Bookmark this address on your computer, and visit this newly-launched website today. With the E-Learning Center, knowledge of Chinese Metaphysics is a mere 'click' away!

Our E-Learning Center consists of 3 distinct components.

1. Online Courses

These shall comprise of 3 Programs: our Online Feng Shui Program, Online BaZi Program, and Online Mian Xiang Program. Each lesson contains a video lecture, slide presentation and downloadable course notes.

2. MA Live!

With MA Live!, Joey Yap's workshops, tutorials, courses and seminars on various Chinese Metaphysics subjects broadcasted right to your computer screen. Better still, participants will not only get to see and hear Joey talk 'live', but also get to engage themselves directly in the event and more importantly, TALK to Joey via the MA Live! interface. All the benefits of a live class, minus the hassle of actually having to attend one!

3. Video-On-Demand (VOD)

Get immediate streaming-downloads of the Mastery Academy's wide range of educational DVDs, right on your computer screen. No more shipping costs and waiting time to be incurred!

Study at your own pace, and interact with your Instructor and fellow students worldwide… at your own convenience and privacy. With our E-Learning Center, knowledge of Chinese Metaphysics is brought DIRECTLY to you in all its clarity, with illustrated presentations and comprehensive notes expediting your learning curve!

Welcome to the Mastery Academy's E-LEARNING CENTER…YOUR virtual gateway to Chinese Metaphysics mastery!

General References

24 Mountain Reference Table

Gua	Direction		24 Mountains		Degrees
離 Li	South	S1	丙 Bing	Yang Fire	157.6 - 172.5
		S2	午 Wu	Horse (Yang Fire)	172.6 - 187.5
		S3	丁 Ding	Yin Fire	187.6 -202.5
坤 Kun	Southwest	SW1	未 Wei	Goat (Yin Earth)	202.6 - 217.5
		SW2	坤 Kun	Southwest (Earth)	217.6 - 232.5
		SW3	申 Shen	Monkey (Yang Metal)	232.6 - 247.5
兌 Dui	West	W1	庚 Geng	Yang Metal	247.6 - 262.5
		W2	酉 You	Rooster (Yin Metal)	262.6 - 277.5
		W3	辛 Xin	Yin Metal	277.6 - 292.5
乾 Qian	Northwest	NW1	戌 Xu	Dog (Yang Earth)	292.6 - 307.5
		NW2	乾 Qian	Northwest (Metal)	307.6 - 322.5
		NW3	亥 Hai	Pig (Yin Water)	322.6 - 337.5
坎 Kan	North	N1	壬 Ren	Yang Water	337.6 - 352.5
		N2	子 Zi	Rat (Yang Water)	352.6 - 7.5
		N3	癸 Gui	Yin Water	7.6 - 22.5
艮 Gen	Northeast	NE1	丑 Chou	Ox (Yin Earth)	22.6 - 37.5
		NE2	艮 Gen	Northeast (Earth)	37.6 - 52.5
		NE3	寅 Yin	Tiger (Yang Wood)	52.6 - 67.5
震 Zhen	East	E1	甲 Jia	Yang Wood	67.6 - 82.5
		E2	卯 Mao	Rabbit (Yin Wood)	82.6 - 97.5
		E3	乙 Yi	Yin Wood	97.6 - 112.5
巽 Xun	Southeast	SE1	辰 Chen	Dragon (Yang Earth)	112.6 - 127.5
		SE2	巽 Xun	Southeast (Wood)	127.6 -142.5
		SE3	巳 Si	Snake (Yin Fire)	142.6 - 157.5

Grand Duke Reference Table 1900-1959

Year	Grand Duke	Year	Grand Duke	Year	Grand Duke
1900 **Metal Rat** 庚子 *Geng Zi*	子 *Zi* Rat	1920 **Metal Monkey** 庚申 *Geng Shen*	申 *Shen* Monkey	1940 **Metal Dragon** 庚辰 *Geng Chen*	辰 *Chen* Dragon
1901 **Metal Ox** 辛丑 *Xin Chou*	丑 *Chou* Ox	1921 **Metal Rooster** 辛酉 *Xin You*	酉 *You* Rooster	1941 **Metal Snake** 辛巳 *Xin Si*	巳 *Si* Snake
1902 **Water Tiger** 壬寅 *Ren Yin*	寅 *Yin* Tiger	1922 **Water Dog** 壬戌 *Ren Xu*	戌 *Xu* Dog	1942 **Water Horse** 壬午 *Ren Wu*	午 *Wu* Horse
1903 **Water Rabbit** 癸卯 *Gui Mao*	卯 *Mao* Rabbit	1923 **Water Pig** 癸亥 *Gui Hai*	亥 *Hai* Pig	1943 **Water Goat** 癸未 *Gui Wei*	未 *Wei* Goat
1904 **Wood Dragon** 甲辰 *Jia Chen*	辰 *Chen* Dragon	1924 **Wood Rat** 甲子 *Jia Zi*	子 *Zi* Rat	1944 **Wood Monkey** 甲申 *Jia Shen*	申 *Shen* Monkey
1905 **Wood Snake** 乙巳 *Yi Si*	巳 *Si* Snake	1925 **Wood Ox** 乙丑 *Yi Chou*	丑 *Chou* Ox	1945 **Wood Rooster** 乙酉 *Yi You*	酉 *You* Rooster
1906 **Fire Horse** 丙午 *Bing Wu*	午 *Wu* Horse	1926 **Fire Tiger** 丙寅 *Bing Yin*	寅 *Yin* Tiger	1946 **Fire Dog** 丙戌 *Bing Xu*	戌 *Xu* Dog
1907 **Fire Goat** 丁未 *Ding Wei*	未 *Wei* Goat	1927 **Fire Rabbit** 丁卯 *Ding Mao*	卯 *Mao* Rabbit	1947 **Fire Pig** 丁亥 *Ding Hai*	亥 *Hai* Pig
1908 **Earth Monkey** 戊申 *Wu Shen*	申 *Shen* Monkey	1928 **Earth Dragon** 戊辰 *Wu Chen*	辰 *Chen* Dragon	1948 **Earth Rat** 戊子 *Wu Zi*	子 *Zi* Rat
1909 **Earth Rooster** 己酉 *Ji You*	酉 *You* Rooster	1929 **Earth Snake** 己巳 *Ji Si*	巳 *Si* Snake	1949 **Earth Ox** 己丑 *Ji Chou*	丑 *Chou* Ox
1910 **Metal Dog** 庚戌 *Geng Xu*	戌 *Xu* Dog	1930 **Metal Horse** 庚午 *Geng Wu*	午 *Wu* Horse	1950 **Metal Tiger** 庚寅 *Geng Yin*	寅 *Yin* Tiger
1911 **Metal Pig** 辛亥 *Xin Hai*	亥 *Hai* Pig	1931 **Metal Goat** 辛未 *Xin Wei*	未 *Wei* Goat	1951 **Metal Rabbit** 辛卯 *Xin Mao*	卯 *Mao* Rabbit
1912 **Water Rat** 壬子 *Ren Zi*	子 *Zi* Rat	1932 **Water Monkey** 壬申 *Ren Shen*	申 *Shen* Monkey	1952 **Water Dragon** 壬辰 *Ren Chen*	辰 *Chen* Dragon
1913 **Water Ox** 癸丑 *Gui Chou*	丑 *Chou* Ox	1933 **Water Rooster** 癸酉 *Gui You*	酉 *You* Rooster	1953 **Water Snake** 癸巳 *Gui Si*	巳 *Si* Snake
1914 **Wood Tiger** 甲寅 *Jia Yin*	寅 *Yin* Tiger	1934 **Wood Dog** 甲戌 *Jia Xu*	戌 *Xu* Dog	1954 **Wood Horse** 甲午 *Jia Wu*	午 *Wu* Horse
1915 **Wood Rabbit** 乙卯 *Yi Mao*	卯 *Mao* Rabbit	1935 **Wood Pig** 乙亥 *Yi Hai*	亥 *Hai* Pig	1955 **Wood Goat** 乙未 *Yi Wei*	未 *Wei* Goat
1916 **Fire Dragon** 丙辰 *Bing Chen*	辰 *Chen* Dragon	1936 **Fire Rat** 丙子 *Bing Zi*	子 *Zi* Rat	1956 **Fire Monkey** 丙申 *Bing Shen*	申 *Shen* Monkey
1917 **Fire Snake** 丁巳 *Ding Si*	巳 *Si* Snake	1937 **Fire Ox** 丁丑 *Ding Chou*	丑 *Chou* Ox	1957 **Fire Rooster** 丁酉 *Ding You*	酉 *You* Rooster
1918 **Earth Horse** 戊午 *Wu Wu*	午 *Wu* Horse	1938 **Earth Tiger** 戊寅 *Wu Yin*	寅 *Yin* Tiger	1958 **Earth Dog** 戊戌 *Wu Xu*	戌 *Xu* Dog
1919 **Earth Goat** 己未 *Ji Wei*	未 *Wei* Goat	1939 **Earth Rabbit** 己卯 *Ji Mao*	卯 *Mao* Rabbit	1959 **Earth Pig** 己亥 *Ji Hai*	亥 *Hai* Pig

Granduke Reference Table 1960-2019

Year	Grand Duke	Year	Grand Duke	Year	Grand Duke
1960 **Metal Rat** 庚子 *Geng Zi*	子 Zi Rat	1980 **Metal Monkey** 庚申 *Geng Shen*	申 Shen Monkey	2000 **Metal Dragon** 庚辰 *Geng Chen*	辰 Chen Dragon
1961 **Metal Ox** 辛丑 *Xin Chou*	丑 Chou Ox	1981 **Metal Rooster** 辛酉 *Xin You*	酉 You Rooster	2001 **Metal Snake** 辛巳 *Xin Si*	巳 Si Snake
1962 **Water Tiger** 壬寅 *Ren Yin*	寅 Yin Tiger	1982 **Water Dog** 壬戌 *Ren Xu*	戌 Xu Dog	2002 **Water Horse** 壬午 *Ren Wu*	午 Wu Horse
1963 **Water Rabbit** 癸卯 *Gui Mao*	卯 Mao Rabbit	1983 **Water Pig** 癸亥 *Gui Hai*	亥 Hai Pig	2003 **Water Goat** 癸未 *Gui Wei*	未 Wei Goat
1964 **Wood Dragon** 甲辰 *Jia Chen*	辰 Chen Dragon	1984 **Wood Rat** 甲子 *Jia Zi*	子 Zi Rat	2004 **Wood Monkey** 甲申 *Jia Shen*	申 Shen Monkey
1965 **Wood Snake** 乙巳 *Yi Si*	巳 Si Snake	1985 **Wood Ox** 乙丑 *Yi Chou*	丑 Chou Ox	2005 **Wood Rooster** 乙酉 *Yi You*	酉 You Rooster
1966 **Fire Horse** 丙午 *Bing Wu*	午 Wu Horse	1986 **Fire Tiger** 丙寅 *Bing Yin*	寅 Yin Tiger	2006 **Fire Dog** 丙戌 *Bing Xu*	戌 Xu Dog
1967 **Fire Goat** 丁未 *Ding Wei*	未 Wei Goat	1987 **Fire Rabbit** 丁卯 *Ding Mao*	卯 Mao Rabbit	2007 **Fire Pig** 丁亥 *Ding Hai*	亥 Hai Pig
1968 **Earth Monkey** 戊申 *Wu Shen*	申 Shen Monkey	1988 **Earth Dragon** 戊辰 *Wu Chen*	辰 Chen Dragon	2008 **Earth Rat** 戊子 *Wu Zi*	子 Zi Rat
1969 **Earth Rooster** 己酉 *Ji You*	酉 You Rooster	1989 **Earth Snake** 己巳 *Ji Si*	巳 Si Snake	2009 **Earth Ox** 己丑 *Ji Chou*	丑 Chou Ox
1970 **Metal Dog** 庚戌 *Geng Xu*	戌 Xu Dog	1990 **Metal Horse** 庚午 *Geng Wu*	午 Wu Horse	2010 **Metal Tiger** 庚寅 *Geng Yin*	寅 Yin Tiger
1971 **Metal Pig** 辛亥 *Xin Hai*	亥 Hai Pig	1991 **Metal Goat** 辛未 *Xin Wei*	未 Wei Goat	2011 **Metal Rabbit** 辛卯 *Xin Mao*	卯 Mao Rabbit
1972 **Water Rat** 壬子 *Ren Zi*	子 Zi Rat	1992 **Water Monkey** 壬申 *Ren Shen*	申 Shen Monkey	2012 **Water Dragon** 壬辰 *Ren Chen*	辰 Chen Dragon
1973 **Water Ox** 癸丑 *Gui Chou*	丑 Chou Ox	1993 **Water Rooster** 癸酉 *Gui You*	酉 You Rooster	2013 **Water Snake** 癸巳 *Gui Si*	巳 Si Snake
1974 **Wood Tiger** 甲寅 *Jia Yin*	寅 Yin Tiger	1994 **Wood Dog** 甲戌 *Jia Xu*	戌 Xu Dog	2014 **Wood Horse** 甲午 *Jia Wu*	午 Wu Horse
1975 **Wood Rabbit** 乙卯 *Yi Mao*	卯 Mao Rabbit	1995 **Wood Pig** 乙亥 *Yi Hai*	亥 Hai Pig	2015 **Wood Goat** 乙未 *Yi Wei*	未 Wei Goat
1976 **Fire Dragon** 丙辰 *Bing Chen*	辰 Chen Dragon	1996 **Fire Rat** 丙子 *Bing Zi*	子 Zi Rat	2016 **Fire Monkey** 丙申 *Bing Shen*	申 Shen Monkey
1977 **Fire Snake** 丁巳 *Ding Si*	巳 Si Snake	1997 **Fire Ox** 丁丑 *Ding Chou*	丑 Chou Ox	2017 **Fire Rooster** 丁酉 *Ding You*	酉 You Rooster
1978 **Earth Horse** 戊午 *Wu Wu*	午 Wu Horse	1998 **Earth Tiger** 戊寅 *Wu Yin*	寅 Yin Tiger	2018 **Earth Dog** 戊戌 *Wu Xu*	戌 Xu Dog
1979 **Earth Goat** 己未 *Ji Wei*	未 Wei Goat	1999 **Earth Rabbit** 己卯 *Ji Mao*	卯 Mao Rabbit	2019 **Earth Pig** 己亥 *Ji Hai*	亥 Hai Pig

Granduke Reference Table 2020-2079

Year	Grand Duke	Year	Grand Duke	Year	Grand Duke
2020 **Metal Rat** 庚子 *Geng Zi*	子 *Zi* Rat	2040 **Metal Monkey** 庚申 *Geng Shen*	申 *Shen* Monkey	2060 **Metal Dragon** 庚辰 *Geng Chen*	辰 *Chen* Dragon
2021 **Metal Ox** 辛丑 *Xin Chou*	丑 *Chou* Ox	2041 **Metal Rooster** 辛酉 *Xin You*	酉 *You* Rooster	2061 **Metal Snake** 辛巳 *Xin Si*	巳 *Si* Snake
2022 **Water Tiger** 壬寅 *Ren Yin*	寅 *Yin* Tiger	2042 **Water Dog** 壬戌 *Ren Xu*	戌 *Xu* Dog	2062 **Water Horse** 壬午 *Ren Wu*	午 *Wu* Horse
2023 **Water Rabbit** 癸卯 *Gui Mao*	卯 *Mao* Rabbit	2043 **Water Pig** 癸亥 *Gui Hai*	亥 *Hai* Pig	2063 **Water Goat** 癸未 *Gui Wei*	未 *Wei* Goat
2024 **Wood Dragon** 甲辰 *Jia Chen*	辰 *Chen* Dragon	2044 **Wood Rat** 甲子 *Jia Zi*	子 *Zi* Rat	2064 **Wood Monkey** 甲申 *Jia Shen*	申 *Shen* Monkey
2025 **Wood Snake** 乙巳 *Yi Si*	巳 *Si* Snake	2045 **Wood Ox** 乙丑 *Yi Chou*	丑 *Chou* Ox	2065 **Wood Rooster** 乙酉 *Yi You*	酉 *You* Rooster
2026 **Fire Horse** 丙午 *Bing Wu*	午 *Wu* Horse	2046 **Fire Tiger** 丙寅 *Bing Yin*	寅 *Yin* Tiger	2066 **Fire Dog** 丙戌 *Bing Xu*	戌 *Xu* Dog
2027 **Fire Goat** 丁未 *Ding Wei*	未 *Wei* Goat	2047 **Fire Rabbit** 丁卯 *Ding Mao*	卯 *Mao* Rabbit	2067 **Fire Pig** 丁亥 *Ding Hai*	亥 *Hai* Pig
2028 **Earth Monkey** 戊申 *Wu Shen*	申 *Shen* Monkey	2048 **Earth Dragon** 戊辰 *Wu Chen*	辰 *Chen* Dragon	2068 **Earth Rat** 戊子 *Wu Zi*	子 *Zi* Rat
2029 **Earth Rooster** 己酉 *Ji You*	酉 *You* Rooster	2049 **Earth Snake** 己巳 *Ji Si*	巳 *Si* Snake	2069 **Earth Ox** 己丑 *Ji Chou*	丑 *Chou* Ox
2030 **Metal Dog** 庚戌 *Geng Xu*	戌 *Xu* Dog	2050 **Metal Horse** 庚午 *Geng Wu*	午 *Wu* Horse	2070 **Metal Tiger** 庚寅 *Geng Yin*	寅 *Yin* Tiger
2031 **Metal Pig** 辛亥 *Xin Hai*	亥 *Hai* Pig	2051 **Metal Goat** 辛未 *Xin Wei*	未 *Wei* Goat	2071 **Metal Rabbit** 辛卯 *Xin Mao*	卯 *Mao* Rabbit
2032 **Water Rat** 壬子 *Ren Zi*	子 *Zi* Rat	2052 **Water Monkey** 壬申 *Ren Shen*	申 *Shen* Monkey	2072 **Water Dragon** 壬辰 *Ren Chen*	辰 *Chen* Dragon
2033 **Water Ox** 癸丑 *Gui Chou*	丑 *Chou* Ox	2053 **Water Rooster** 癸酉 *Gui You*	酉 *You* Rooster	2073 **Water Snake** 癸巳 *Gui Si*	巳 *Si* Snake
2034 **Wood Tiger** 甲寅 *Jia Yin*	寅 *Yin* Tiger	2054 **Wood Dog** 甲戌 *Jia Xu*	戌 *Xu* Dog	2074 **Wood Horse** 甲午 *Jia Wu*	午 *Wu* Horse
2035 **Wood Rabbit** 乙卯 *Yi Mao*	卯 *Mao* Rabbit	2055 **Wood Pig** 乙亥 *Yi Hai*	亥 *Hai* Pig	2075 **Wood Goat** 乙未 *Yi Wei*	未 *Wei* Goat
2036 **Fire Dragon** 丙辰 *Bing Chen*	辰 *Chen* Dragon	2056 **Fire Rat** 丙子 *Bing Zi*	子 *Zi* Rat	2076 **Fire Monkey** 丙申 *Bing Shen*	申 *Shen* Monkey
2037 **Fire Snake** 丁巳 *Ding Si*	巳 *Si* Snake	2057 **Fire Ox** 丁丑 *Ding Chou*	丑 *Chou* Ox	2077 **Fire Rooster** 丁酉 *Ding You*	酉 *You* Rooster
2038 **Earth Horse** 戊午 *Wu Wu*	午 *Wu* Horse	2058 **Earth Tiger** 戊寅 *Wu Yin*	寅 *Yin* Tiger	2078 **Earth Dog** 戊戌 *Wu Xu*	戌 *Xu* Dog
2039 **Earth Goat** 己未 *Ji Wei*	未 *Wei* Goat	2059 **Earth Rabbit** 己卯 *Ji Mao*	卯 *Mao* Rabbit	2079 **Earth Pig** 己亥 *Ji Hai*	亥 *Hai* Pig

Joey Yap's San Yuan Luo Pan

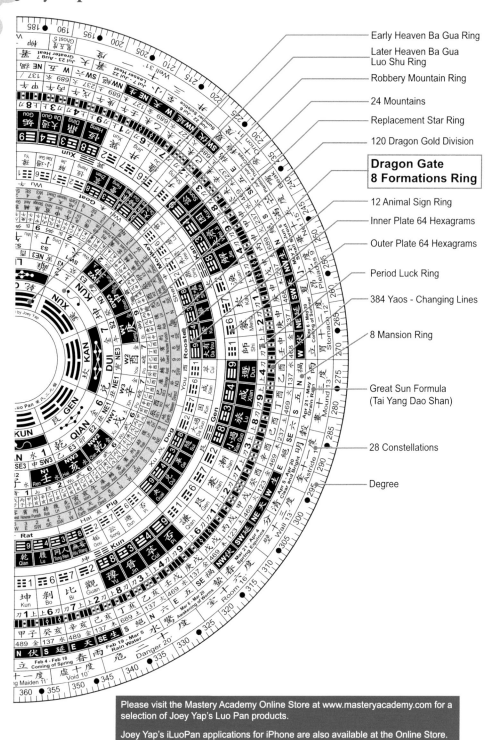

- Early Heaven Ba Gua Ring
- Later Heaven Ba Gua Luo Shu Ring
- Robbery Mountain Ring
- 24 Mountains
- Replacement Star Ring
- 120 Dragon Gold Division
- **Dragon Gate 8 Formations Ring**
- 12 Animal Sign Ring
- Inner Plate 64 Hexagrams
- Outer Plate 64 Hexagrams
- Period Luck Ring
- 384 Yaos - Changing Lines
- 8 Mansion Ring
- Great Sun Formula (Tai Yang Dao Shan)
- 28 Constellations
- Degree

1. Qian Formation 乾局

1. Qian Formation

Sitting : **Qian 乾**   Facing : **Xun 巽**

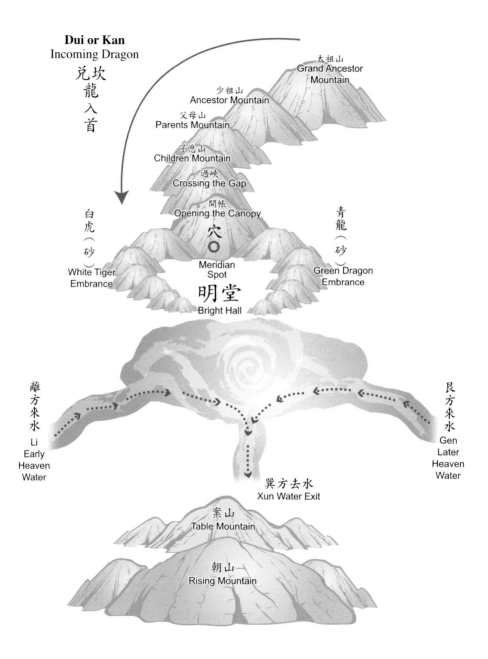

Dui or Kan
Incoming Dragon
兌坎龍入首

太祖山
Grand Ancestor
Mountain

少祖山
Ancestor Mountain

父母山
Parents Mountain

子息山
Children Mountain

過峽
Crossing the Gap

開帳
Opening the Canopy

白虎（砂）
White Tiger
Embrace

穴〇
Meridian
Spot

青龍（砂）
Green Dragon
Embrace

明堂
Bright Hall

離方來水
Li
Early
Heaven
Water

艮方來水
Gen
Later
Heaven
Water

巽方去水
Xun Water Exit

案山
Table Mountain

朝山
Rising Mountain

1.	**Qian Formation**			
	Sitting :	**Qian 乾**	Facing :	**Xun 巽**

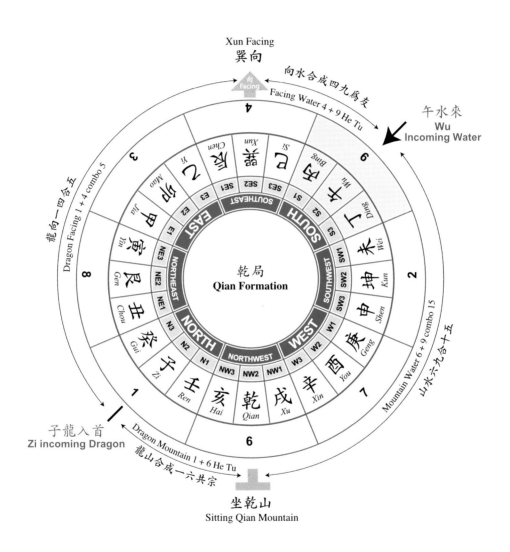

Xun Facing
巽向

向水合成四九爲友
Facing Water 4 + 9 He Tu

午水來
Wu
Incoming Water

乾局
Qian Formation

龍向一四合五
Dragon Facing 1 + 4 combo 5

山水六九合十五
Mountain Water 6 + 9 combo 15

子龍入首
Zi incoming Dragon

龍山合成一六共宗
Dragon Mountain 1 + 6 He Tu

坐乾山
Sitting Qian Mountain

1. Qian Formation

Sitting : **Qian 乾**　　　　Facing : **Xun 巽**

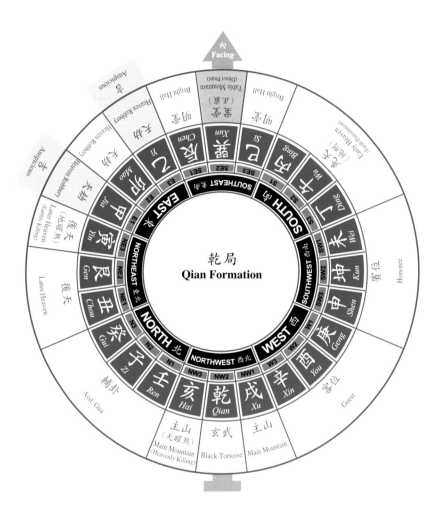

乾局
Qian Formation

1. Qian Formation

Auspicious : **Jia** 甲, **Yi** 乙

If the Internal Water (內程水) is located on the left, the left side of the property will enjoy the best possible luck from this scenario, and prosper accordingly. Similarly, should the Internal Water (內程水) happen to be located on the right, the right side of the property concerned will benefit accordingly. Water Exiting Xun (埕水放巽位去) would, however, produce the best possible outcomes; followed by Water Released and Exiting through a Yi Mouth (水放乙出口). A Jia Exit (放甲) will bring about average outcomes. One should, however, be mindful of a Jia Exit, Combined with Water Exiting Yin寅 (放甲兼寅而去), as it is the harbinger of inauspicious outcomes, which will also see female family members being afflicted by poor health.

An External Structure, Exiting through the Xun Direction (外局放巽位出) produces what is known as a Qian Mountain (乾山). This is the primary and most important Water Mouth, as it brings about auspicious outcomes that will prosper each and every member of a family. Similarly, Water Flowing and Exiting through a Yi Position (水流乙位出口) will also bring about extremely auspicious outcomes. One should, however, ensure that a Jia Exit (出甲) does not combine with Seaming Yin (Tiger) (兼寅) sector.

2. Qian Formation

Sitting : **Qian 乾**   Facing : **Xun 巽**

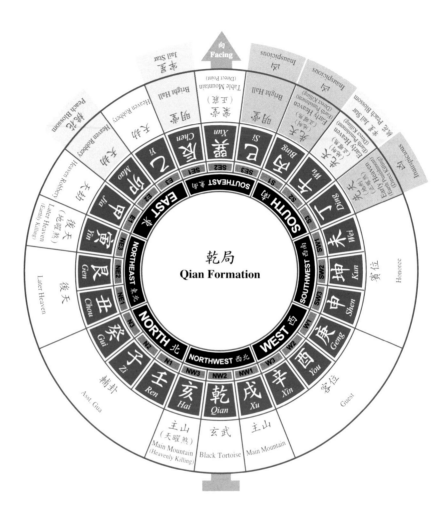

乾局
Qian Formation

2.	Qian Formation			
Inauspicious :	Si 巳，Bing 丙，Ding 丁		Peach Blossom :	Mao 卯，Wu 午

Internal (內) and External Structure Water (外局水), as well as Water passing by Li Gua (水流離卦) produce what is known as the Clashing Out Early Heaven (破先天) Formation. This is an extremely inauspicious scenario, which indicates harm befalling the children in the family, as well as the possibility of a miscarriage. A Bing Water Mouth (丙口) would be most unfavorable to the second son, while a Wu Water Mouth (午口) would be unfavorable to every son and female member of the family. The latter is also the harbinger of legal problems, and harm befalling one's father. Likewise, a Ding Water Mouth (丁口) would affect the third son most adversely.

On the contrary, a Mao Exit (卯) would be most favorable to the eldest son. However, should it coincide with a Grand Duke Punishment and Clash (太歲刑沖), one will be troubled by problems. In any case, a Chen Exit (辰) would bring about unfavorable outcomes to the second son, including imprisonment and chronic illnesses. Similarly, a Si Exit (巳) would be most unfavorable to the youngest son in the family.

3. Qian Formation

| Sitting : | **Qian 乾** | Facing : | **Xun 巽** |

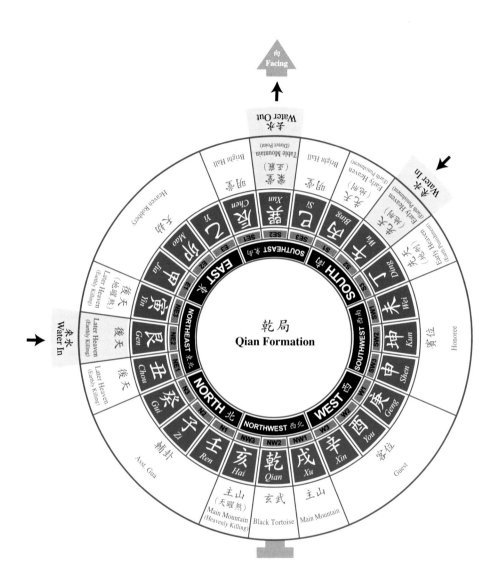

3.	Qian Formation		
Water In :	**Gen** 艮, **Wu** 午	Water Out :	**Xun** 巽

The presence of Receiving Early Heaven Li Gua Water (先天離卦水朝來) is an auspicious sign, which brings about favorable outcomes to all family members. Combined with Incoming Later Heaven Gen Water, Flowing towards the Xun Direction (後天艮水來巽方而去), one will be blessed with a large family, with each and every member of the family prospering. Where Xun 巽 is located toward the right side of Chen 辰, the outcomes would be most favorable to the eldest and third sons. However, should the Water exit directly from the Central Hall (堂中), one's luck will eventually decline. It would therefore be better for the Water Exit Position (出水處) to be either sheltered, or for the Water to flow along a curving course. A Xun Exit (巽) constitutes the primary and most important Water Mouth, as it brings about prosperity and fame for each and every member of the family.

4. Qian Formation

Sitting : **Qian 乾**　　　Facing : **Xun 巽**

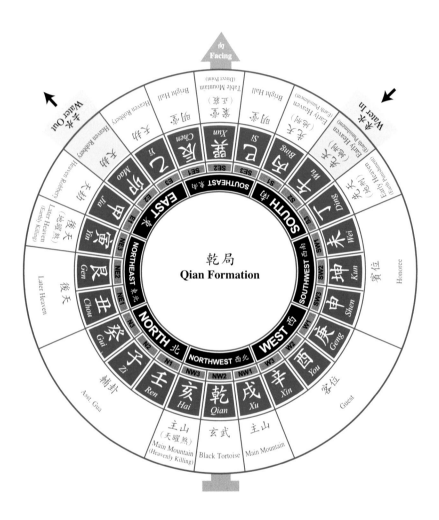

4.	**Qian Formation**		
Water In :	**Wu** 午	Water Out :	**Mao** 卯

Water from Li, Leaving Zhen (離水來震水去) produces what is known as 'rebellious water'. While it brings about a large, wealthy family, it also results in a Diminishing Void Total Disaster (消亡敗絕), whereby the family's luck will eventually decline. If this 'rebellious water' is Receive and Crosses Bright Hall (收來過堂), the children in the family will tend to behave in a rebellious, disobedient manner. Such a Formation may provide one with good beginner's luck during the initial stages of an endeavor, although such luck will eventually run out. Furthermore, it could also result in relationship problems, as well as loss of wealth.

5. Qian Formation

| Sitting : | **Qian** 乾 | Facing : | **Xun** 巽 |

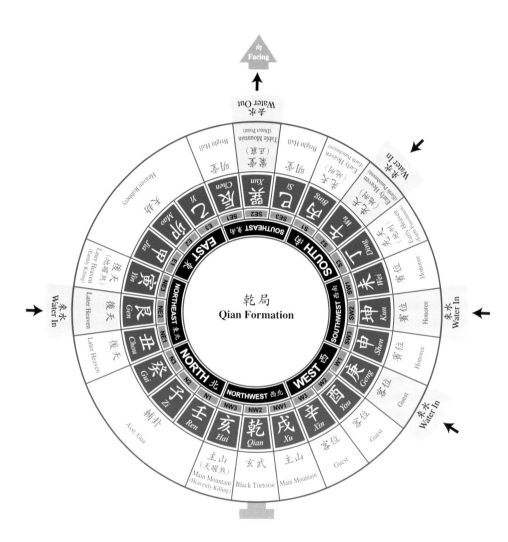

5.	Qian Formation		
Water In :	**Wu** 午，**Kun** 坤，**Geng** 庚，**Gen** 艮	Water Out :	**Xun** 巽

Incoming Guest Water, Combine with Later Heaven Water (賓客水來，轉合先後天) is an extremely auspicious Formation, also known as the Guest Water Assisted Structure (賓客助主). Where such a Formation is seen, one will be blessed with a large family and prosperity.

6. Qian Formation

Sitting : **Qian 乾**   Facing : **Xun 巽**

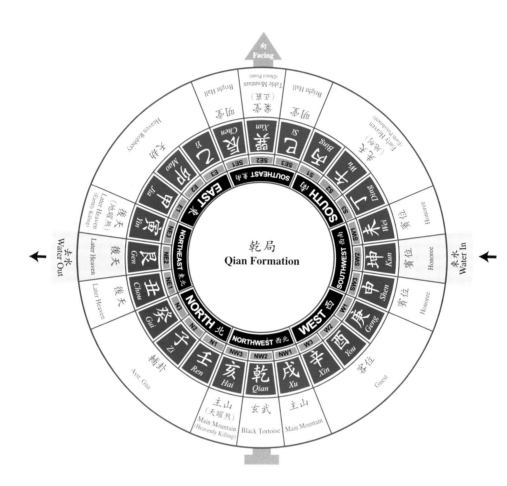

乾局
Qian Formation

6.	Qian Formation			
Water In :	**Kun** 坤		Water Out :	**Gen** 艮

Incoming Guest Water, passing through the Bright Hall (賓客水收來過堂) and Shooting through Early Heaven or Later Heaven (囚射先天或後天) produce what is known as Internal Supporting External (內益外) Formation. This is an extremely ominous or inauspicious scenario. Where a Shooting Through Early Heaven (射破先天) Formation is seen, one may have to adopt children, or be able to sire an only son, or contend with one's son-in-law becoming part of one's family. On the other hand, however, one's daughter's family shall prosper.

7. Qian Formation

| Sitting : | **Qian** 乾 | Facing : | **Xun** 巽 |

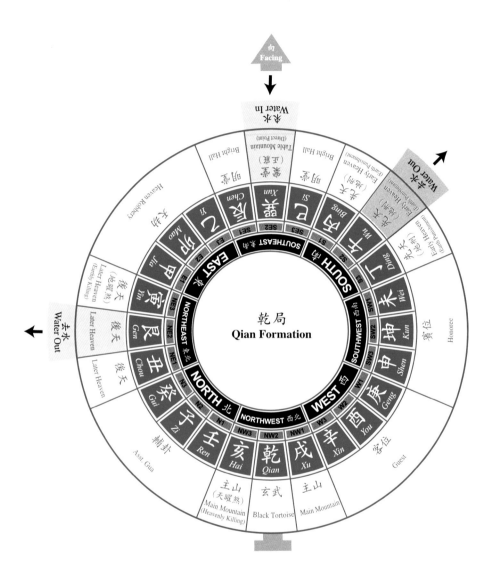

乾局
Qian Formation

7.	Qian Formation		
Water In :	**Xun** 巽	Water Out :	**Gen** 艮，**Wu** 午

Receiving Guest and Honorary Water (堂劫巽卦水來) is also known as Piercing Heart Water (穿心水). This is an extremely inauspicious scenario, as it is the harbinger of heart disease, as well as the possibility of a sudden death in the household. Water that Passes through Gen (水歸艮而去) is another undesirable scenario, as it could result in both male and female family members behaving in a sexually immoral or lascivious manner, or a nasty divorce. Meanwhile, Receiving Xun Gua Water, Passing through the Li Direction (巽卦水來，歸離方去) is known as Clashing Out Early Heaven (破先天) Formation. It indicates the possibility of harm befalling male family members.

8. Qian Formation

Sitting : **Qian 乾**   Facing : **Xun 巽**

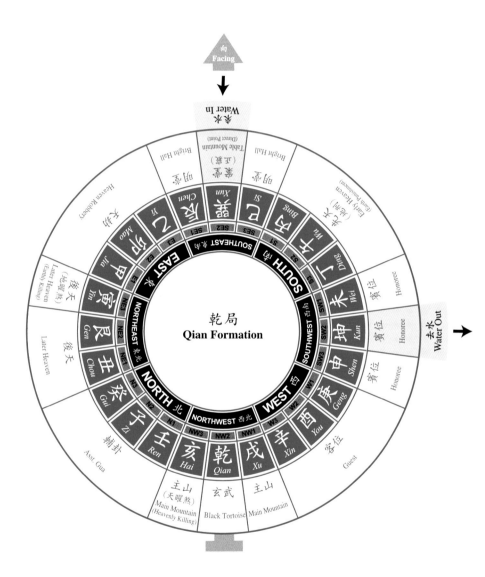

乾局
Qian Formation

8.	Qian Formation		
Water In :	**Xun** 巽	Water Out :	**Kun** 坤

Water from Xun, Passing through Kun (巽水來歸坤而去) brings about a Diminishing Void Total Disaster Water Formation (消亡敗絕水), which in turn, could cause one's family to disintegrate and become disunited. Another inauspicious scenario is Water from Chen (辰水來); which results in a Combined Punishment Water Formation (刑戮水) and Weakness in Later Heaven position (痼疾水). It indicates the possibility of spiritual disturbance, as well as being killed during a robbery or in an accident. As its name implies, it is also the harbinger of chronic or nagging ailments, deafness, muteness, and lip deformities. Similarly, Water from Yi and Chen (乙辰水來) could result in one being crushed to death by a huge log or heavy rock. Furthermore, the presence of a lock-shaped mountain or robe-like road toward the Chen 辰 direction indicates the possibility of one dying in prison.

Water from Si (巳水來) is equally undesirable, as it could result in one's reputation being tarnished, as well as cause one to behave in a lascivious or sexually immoral manner.

9. Qian Formation

Sitting : **Qian 乾**   Facing : **Xun 巽**

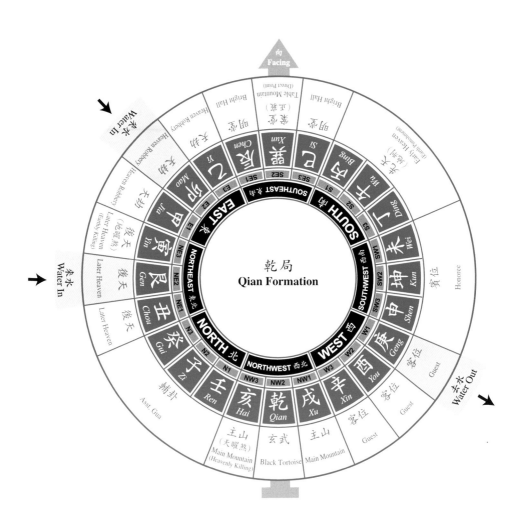

乾局
Qian Formation

9.	Qian Formation			
	Water In :	**Mao** 卯 ，**Gen** 艮	Water Out :	**Geng** 庚

Incoming Heavenly Robbery Zhen Water Joins with Later Heaven Gen Water (天劫震水來會合後天艮水) is also known Water flowing out Guest Position (出客 賓位去). This is an auspicious scenario, as it indicates that one's family members shall be wealthy, outstanding and robust in their pursuits and endeavors. One should, however, be mindful of Incoming Heavenly Robbery Water (天劫水來), as it is the harbinger of ailments that lead to the coughing up of blood, chronic illnesses, as well as the possibility of meeting with a fatal accident.

10. Qian Formation

| Sitting : | **Qian** 乾 | Facing : | **Xun** 巽 |

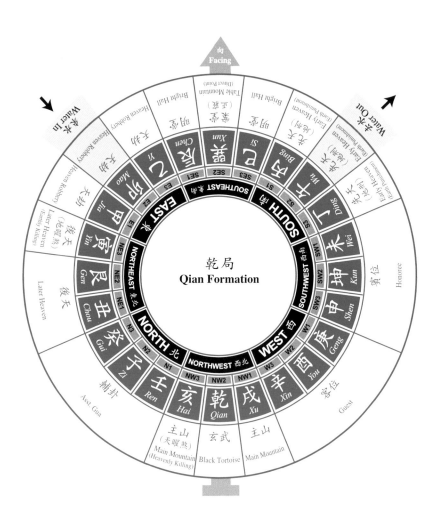

10.	Qian Formation		
Water In :	**Mao** 卯	Water Out :	**Wu** 午

Similarly, Water from Zhen, Exiting through Li Gua (震水來出離卦而去), which is known as a Clashing Out Early Heaven (破先天) Formation, is another inauspicious scenario. It indicates the possibility of harm befalling family members, where they could also pass away at a relatively young age. As such Water is also known to be 'Rebellious Water', it will result in a Diminishing Void Total Disaster Formation (消亡敗絕), which in turn, become the harbinger of disputes and arguments straining family ties, which may cause a rift between siblings. Obviously, such incidents lead to the eventual break-up of family.

Water from Jia (甲水來) is equally ominous, as it indicates the possibility of a family member committing suicide by hanging him or herself, or being crushed to death by a log or rock. Furthermore, incoming Water from either Mao 卯 or Wu 午 could lead to insanity, mental problems as well as a suicide in the family. More specifically, Mao 卯 represents female family members, while Wu 午 represents male family members.

Another inauspicious sign is Water from Jia (甲水來), which could bring about unfortunate consequences such as insanity, crippling disablements, physical deformities or worse still, meeting with a fatal accident.

11. Qian Formation

| Sitting : | **Qian** 乾 | Facing : | **Xun** 巽 |

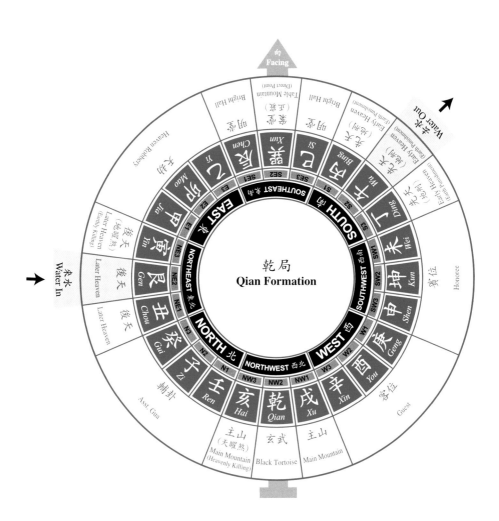

乾局
Qian Formation

11.	Qian Formation		
Water In :	**Gen** 艮	Water Out :	**Wu** 午

Water from Gen, Leaving Li (艮水來離水去) is also known as Clashing Out Early Heaven (破先天). This is an inauspicious scenario, as it indicates the possibility of harm befalling male family members, where they could also pass away at a relatively young age. One may even be unfortunate enough to sire an only son, or worse still, pass away without leaving a son behind to carry on the family name. A Bing Water Exit (丙) would be most unfavorable to the second son, while a Wu Water Exit (午) would affect the eldest son most adversely. Similarly, a Ding Exit (丁) would be most detrimental to the youngest son. On the contrary, should Water converge and be 'contained' at Li 離, one's family and descendents shall prosper.

In any case, the preceding Formation could result in debauchery or debauched behavior, and also affect one's career prospects in an adverse manner.

12. Qian Formation

| Sitting : | **Qian 乾** | Facing : | **Xun 巽** |

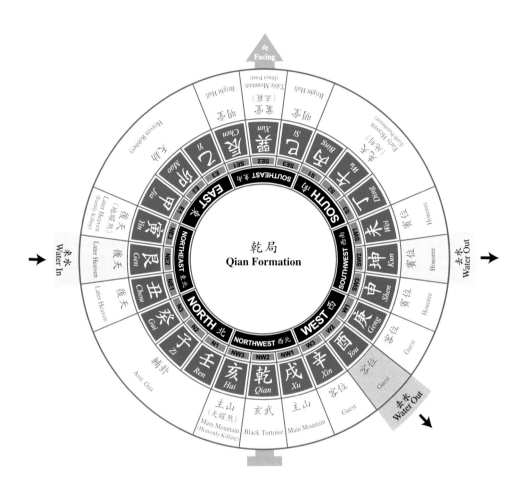

12.	Qian Formation		
Water In :	**Gen** 艮	Water Out :	**Kun** 坤，**You** 酉

Water from Gen, Leaving Kun (艮水來坤水去) produces what is known as a Borrows the Direct Point (借竅) Formation. This is an auspicious scenario, as it brings about wealth and prosperity. It is also known as a Wood City Water Formation (木城水法), and if it Flows Through Dui (流兌), it will bring about equally auspicious outcomes. One should, however, be mindful of this Gua 卦 swerving and losing its balance on the right side, as it could eventually bring about unfortunate outcomes affecting the youngest son.

13. Qian Formation

Sitting :	**Qian 乾**	Facing :	**Xun 巽**

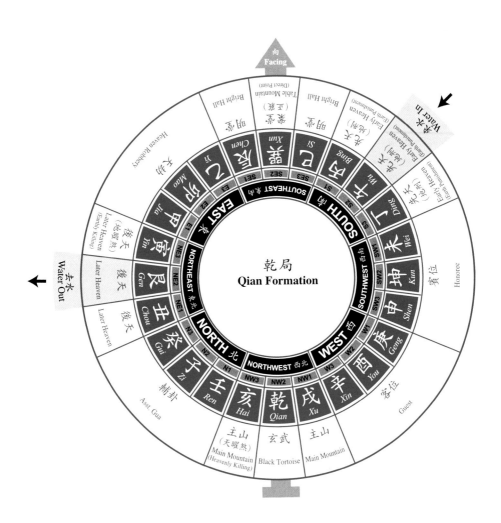

乾局
Qian Formation

13.	**Qian Formation**		
Water In :	**Wu** 午	Water Out :	**Gen** 艮

Incoming Water from Li, Leaving Gen (離水來，艮方去) is also known as Clashing Out Later Heaven (破後天). It brings about inauspicious outcomes, including the possibility of a miscarriage, loss of wealth and divorce. A Chou Exit (丑) would be most unfavorable to the second son, while a Gen Exit (艮) would affect the eldest son most adversely. Similarly, a Yin Exit (寅) would be most detrimental to the third son. Should the Water converge and be 'contained' at Gen 艮, however, one shall prosper and become extremely wealthy. Indeed, one's wife shall bring about good fortunes and wealth to the husband.

14. Qian Formation

| Sitting : | **Qian** 乾 | Facing : | **Xun** 巽 |

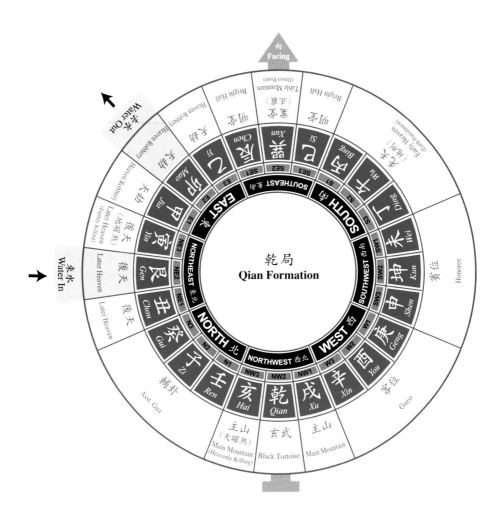

乾局
Qian Formation

14. Qian Formation

Water In : **Gen** 艮   Water Out : **Mao** 卯

Water from Gen, Exiting Through Zhen (艮水來，出震而去) results in what is known as a Diminishing Void Total Disaster Water Formation (消亡敗絕水). Where such a scenario takes place, one's family and descendents will eventually fall apart and become disunited. Should, however, the Water converge and be 'contained' at Zhen 震, one's family shall prosper and become immensely wealthy.

In any case, the preceding Formation indicates that the eldest son may possess differing views and values from his parents and as such, would likely be inclined to strike out on his own, independently.

15. Qian Formation

Sitting : **Qian 乾** | Facing : **Xun 巽**

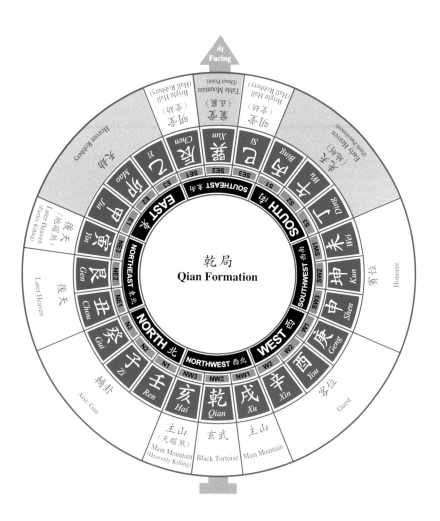

乾局
Qian Formation

15.	Qian Formation			
	Sitting :	Qian 乾	Facing :	Xun 巽

Where an Heavenly Robbery Punishing Hall Robbery 3 Positional Blade (天劫 刑案三位刀) is observed, one should be vigilant so as avoid having a pointed rooftop, pile of rocks, ring or roundabout, sharp or protruding corner, handrail or disused well located within 20 meters from the Bright Hall (明堂). This is because should any of the preceding features be seen within the vicinity, the outcomes would be most inauspicious. Furthermore, the meeting of a "Clashed by Annual Luck (流年地運沖刑)" or "Filling-in the Jupiter Star (填寅歲君)" indicates the possibility of meeting with a car accident, having to undergo medical surgery or suffering from an ailment that leads to the coughing up of blood. More severe possibilities include meeting with a fatal accident, or passing away at a relatively young age.

16. Qian Formation

| Sitting : | **Qian 乾** | Facing : | **Xun 巽** |

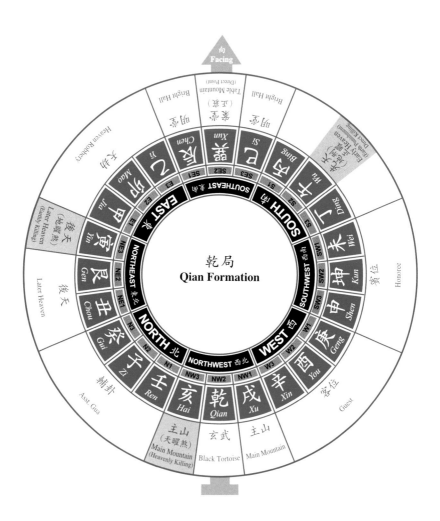

乾局
Qian Formation

16. Qian Formation

Sitting :   **Qian 乾**   Facing :   **Xun 巽**

As Yin 寅, Wu 午 and Hai 亥 constitute the Three Shimmering (三曜), one should take precautionary measures, so as to avoid having a tree, road or sharp corner or junction within the vicinity, as such features could produce inauspicious outcomes. According to the ancient manuscripts, the Shimmering Star (曜星) is the most inauspicious of all, and should these three stars converge upon the same spot, they could cause mental problems and even insanity. In fact, the presence of a tree at such a location will drive a person insane.

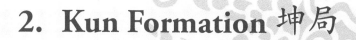

2. Kun Formation 坤局

1. Kun Formation

| Sitting : | **Kun** 坤 | Facing : | **Gen** 艮 |

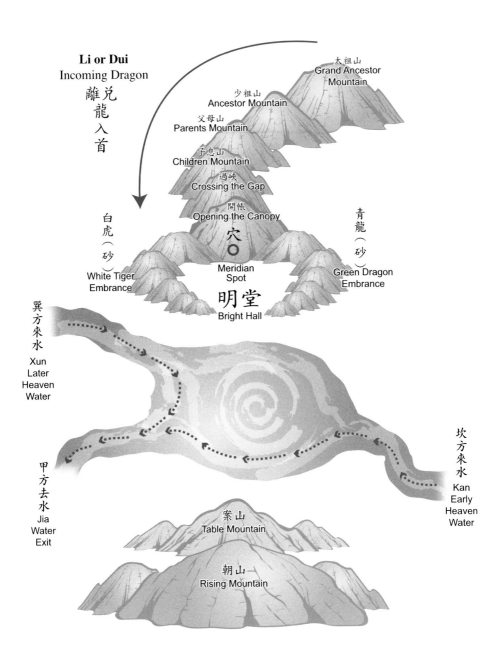

Li or Dui
Incoming Dragon
離兌龍入首

太祖山
Grand Ancestor Mountain

少祖山
Ancestor Mountain

父母山
Parents Mountain

子息山
Children Mountain

過峽
Crossing the Gap

開帳
Opening the Canopy

穴
Meridian Spot

白虎（砂）
White Tiger Embrace

青龍（砂）
Green Dragon Embrace

明堂
Bright Hall

巽方來水
Xun Later Heaven Water

坎方來水
Kan Early Heaven Water

甲方去水
Jia Water Exit

案山
Table Mountain

朝山
Rising Mountain

1. Kun Formation

| Sitting : | **Kun 坤** | Facing : | **Gen 艮** |

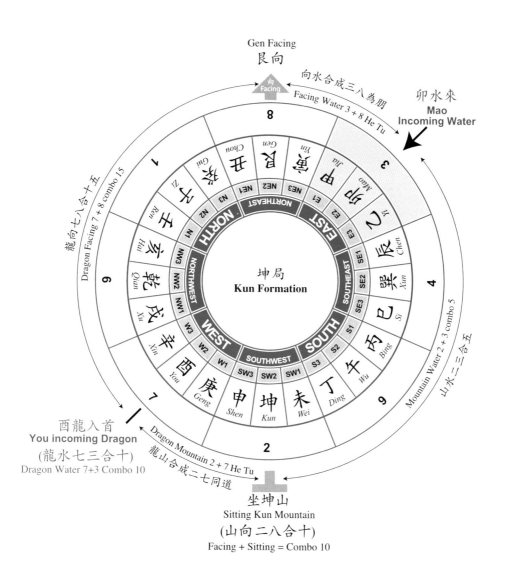

Gen Facing
艮向

向水合成三八為朋
Facing Water 3 + 8 He Tu

卯水來
Mao
Incoming Water

龍向七八合十五
Dragon Facing 7 + 8 combo 15

坤局
Kun Formation

Mountain Water 2 + 3 combo 5
山水二三合五

酉龍入首
You incoming Dragon
(龍水七三合十)
Dragon Water 7+3 Combo 10

Dragon Mountain 2 + 7 He Tu
龍山合成二七同道

坐坤山
Sitting Kun Mountain
(山向二八合十)
Facing + Sitting = Combo 10

1. Kun Formation

Sitting :	**Kun 坤**	Facing :	**Gen 艮**

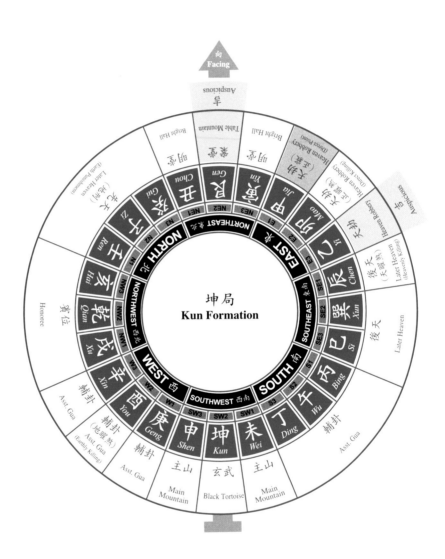

1.	**Kun Formation**
	Auspicious : **Gen** 艮，**Yi** 乙

If the Internal Structure (内局) were to flow to the left side, then the attributes (family members) associated to the left sector would prosper accordingly. Similarly, should the Internal Structure (内局) flow toward the right side, the attributes (family members) associated with the right sector would prosper. Where the Water exits through the Central Bright Hall (堂中), the outcomes would be beneficial to every member of the family; particularly the second son. Likewise, a Gen Exit (艮) would bring about favorable results to everyone in the family. Water exiting from a Jia Exit (甲) would produce outcomes most favorable to the second son, while Water exiting via a Yi Exit (乙) would be most favorable to the youngest son in the family.

External Structure Water (外局水) flowing toward the Jia Water Mouth (甲乙) would also bring about favorable, prosperous outcomes to all family members. In a similar vein, a Yi Exit (出乙) would be equally auspicious in outcome. However, should the External Structure Water (外局水) flow out directly from the Central Bright Hall (堂中), one's luck may appear to be initially good, although the fortunes of the second son in the family will eventually decline. If the External Structure Water (外局水) were to flow toward the Kan 坎 Palace, a scenario known as the Clashing Out Early Heaven (破先天) takes place. Such a scenario would affect the men in the family most adversely, with the second son being particularly susceptible to loneliness and bad luck in life.

2. Kun Formation

Sitting : **Kun 坤**　　Facing : **Gen 艮**

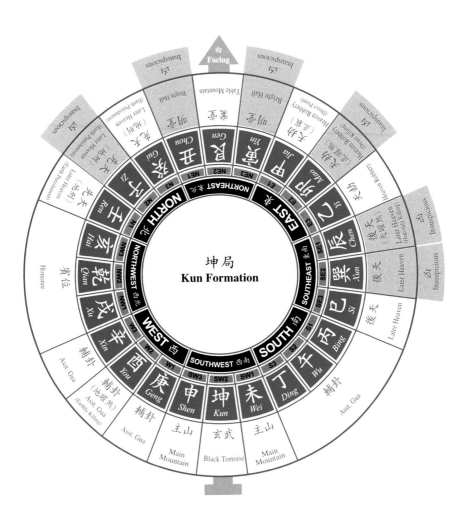

坤局
Kun Formation

2.	Kun Formation
Inauspicious :	Zi 子, Chou 丑, Yin 寅, Mao 卯, Chen 辰, Xun 巽

Internal Structure Mao Exit (內局放卯)

Under such circumstances, the eldest son in the family will be able to enjoy good beginners' luck. Should the Internal Structure Mao Exit (內局放卯) be located at the Shimmering Position (曜位), though, and this very location coincides with one of the Twelve Earthly Branches (地支) during a year with a Grand Duke Punishment and Clash (太歲刑沖), one needs to be mindful of any harm befalling family members, as well as of financial or monetary losses. Likewise, a Chou Exit (出丑) may cause the ladies from the second son's family to suffer from health problems; where they will need to be especially mindful of the consequences of hormonal imbalances. A Yin Exit (出寅) would adversely affect the health of the ladies from the youngest son's family, while a Kan Exit (出坎), which is also known as an Internal Structure Clashing Out Early Heaven (內局破先天) would be generally harmful to one's family members.

External Structure Xun Exit (外局出巽口)

This scenario is also known as the Clashing Out Later Heaven (破後天), which brings about loss of wealth, as well as the possibility of a nasty divorce. The presence of a Chen Exit (出辰) would mean that ladies ought to pay more attention to their health, especially to avoid a miscarriage or physical injury. Where a Xun Gua Clash Out formation (巽卦流破) is present, however, together with a body of water or 'water container' within the vicinity, it might be possible that a man's second marriage will bring him wealth and financial success.

3. Kun Formation

Sitting : **Kun 坤**   Facing : **Gen 艮**

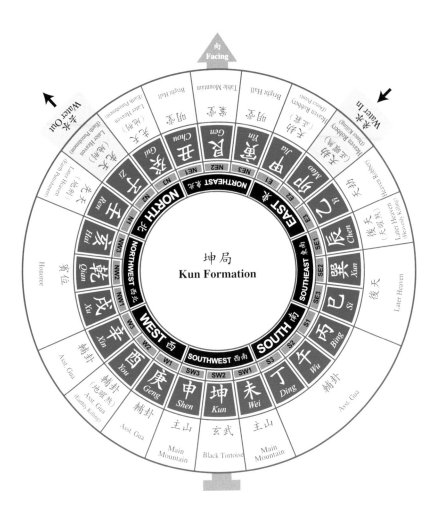

3.	Kun Formation			
Water In :	**Mao** 卯		Water Out :	**Zi** 子

Zhen Gua Water (震卦水) is also known as Incoming Heavenly Robbery Water (天劫水). It is the harbinger of extremely inauspicious things, including ailments that could lead to the coughing up of blood.

Where Water Incoming from Yin and Jia (寅甲水来), one would need to be mindful of any persistent or chronic illnesses, as well as physical handicaps and deformities, such as a family member being hunchbacked.

Incoming Mao Water (卯水来) is an equally inauspicious sign, which could result in outcomes such as a suicide by hanging, being tortured to death, being killed in a robbery or accident, or being afflicted with a terminal or incurable disease. If Water flows from the Chen 辰 direction, this could lead to a Shimmering Act (劫曜) scenario, which indicates the possibility of insanity or mental problems affecting family members. Should Water flow from the Mao 卯 direction, this would result in what is known as Peach Blossom (桃花) Water, whereby the females in the family may be inclined toward behaving in a sexually immoral, coquettish or flirtatious manner. Indeed, Water that flows from Mao (卯水) toward Zi 子 could be an indicator of incest involving the females in the family. Consequently, even the ladies in the family with firm principles and high morals may lean toward unethical or unhealthy relationships.

4. Kun Formation

Sitting : **Kun 坤**　　　　Facing : **Gen 艮**

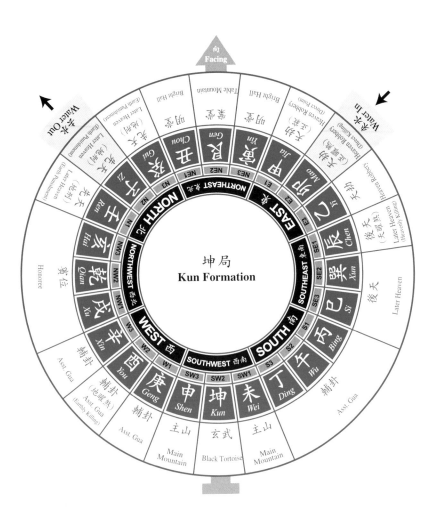

坤局
Kun Formation

4.	Kun Formation			
Water In :	**Mao** 卯		Water Out :	**Zi** 子

'Rebellious Water' is formed when Zhen Incoming Water, Kan Exiting Water (震水來坎水去). Should 'Rebellious Water' coincide with the Clashing Out Early Heaven (破先天) and Earthly Punishment (地刑), this could lead to several unfortunate or inauspicious outcomes. These include younger family members behaving in a rebellious manner, poor health afflicting female family members, the advent of ailments that lead to the coughing up of blood, as well as a tough and challenging life in one's old age. Furthermore, if an old tree is spotted at the Three Directions (三方) of Mao 卯, Chen 辰 and You 酉, one may need to be on the lookout for illnesses or ailments that are not easily detectable.

5. | Kun Formation

| Sitting : | **Kun** 坤 | Facing : | **Gen** 艮 |

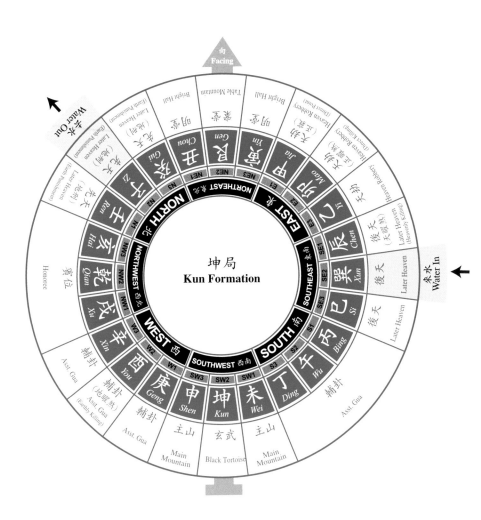

坤局
Kun Formation

5.	**Kun Formation**			
	Water In :	**Xun** 巽	Water Out :	**Zi** 子

Water Coming from Later Heaven Xun Gua, Passing the Bright Hall (後天巽卦水來 過堂) indicates the possibility of having a wealthy, although unintelligent person around.

Incoming Water from Xun (巽水來), as well as Water Leaving Kan (坎水去) will produce what is known as the Clashing Out Early Heaven (破先天), which in turn, would be extremely detrimental or adverse for the males in the family. In fact, a Ren Exit (出壬) would bring about unfavorable outcomes for the second son; a Zi Exit (子) would be unfavorable to the eldest son; while a Gui Exit (癸) would affect the third son most adversely.

6. Kun Formation

| Sitting : | **Kun 坤** | Facing : | **Gen 艮** |

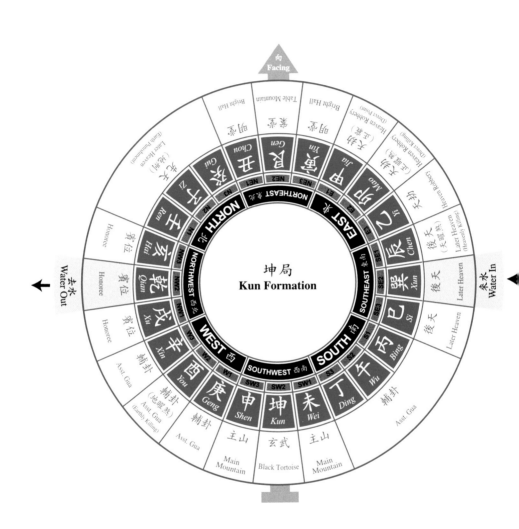

6.	Kun Formation		
Water In :	**Xun** 巽	Water Out :	**Qian** 乾

Incoming Water from Xun (巽水來), Exiting at Qian (乾方去) or otherwise known as a Guest Position (賓位) would, however, bring about favorable wealth luck; although family members will not be privileged enough to benefit from such luck. The presence of Xun Water (巽水) within this Formation might also result in what is known as a Water Clashing Out Kan (破坎方), which is the Early Heaven Position.

7. Kun Formation

| Sitting : | **Kun 坤** | Facing : | **Gen 艮** |

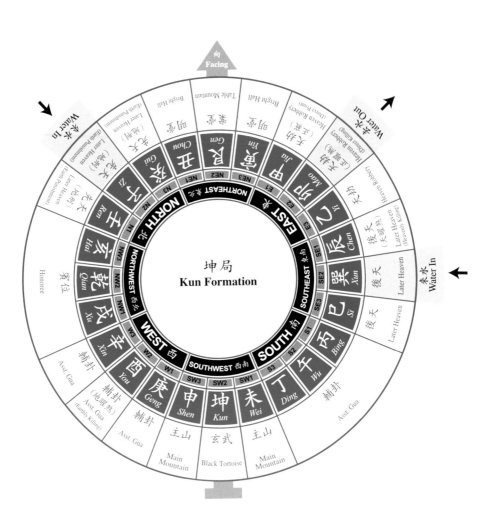

坤局
Kun Formation

7. Kun Formation

Water In : **Zi 子, Xun 巽**   Water Out :   **Mao 卯**

Receiving Early Heaven Kan Water (先天坎卦水來) would bring about extremely auspicious outcomes, indeed, for one's family members. These include the second son in the family prospering and becoming wealthy. Where Kan Water (坎水) and Xun Water (巽水) converge at the Bright Hall (明堂), a Formation known as the 4-1 In the Same Palace (四一同宮) occurs. This indicates that at least someone in the family will rise to a high government position, and become famous. Indeed, such a Formation would complete or consummate Early Heaven (先天) and Later Heaven (後天), whereby one's fame, fortune and status will be perpetually ensured.

Water from the Kan Sector (坎水來), which combines with Xun 巽 to produce a Formation will also bring about two distinct outcomes. Where a Mao Exit (卯) is seen, the outcomes will be extremely auspicious. Similar outcomes may be expected as well, should a Zhen Exit (震) at Jia 甲 and Yi 乙 be present.

8. Kun Formation

| Sitting : | **Kun** 坤 | Facing : | **Gen** 艮 |

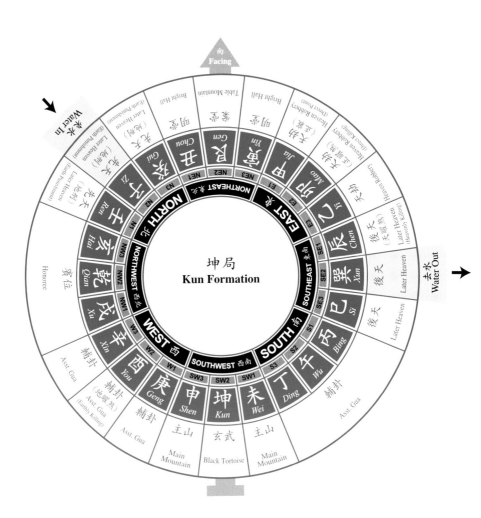

坤局
Kun Formation

8.	Kun Formation			
Water In :	**Zi 子**	Water Out :	**Xun 巽**	

On the contrary, Water from the Kan Sector, Exiting at Xun (坎水來巽水去) will result in what is known as the Clashing Out Later Heaven (破後天) formation. This indicates that one's efforts will encounter complete failure, and nothing one does or undertakes will ever have a lasting effect. Consequently, one will eventually become disheartened, and inclined to keep to oneself. The presence of a Clash Out Later Heaven (流破後天) may also mean each and every generation of one's descendents suffering from poverty and loss of wealth.

9. Kun Formation

Sitting : **Kun 坤**   Facing : **Gen 艮**

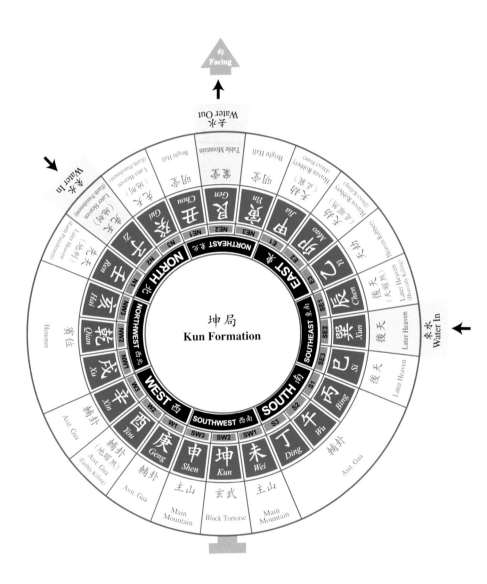

9. Kun Formation

Water In : **Zi 子, Xun 巽**   Water Out :   **Gen 艮**

Receiving Early Heaven Kan Water (先天坎卦水來) would bring about extremely auspicious outcomes, indeed, for one's family members. These include the second son in the family prospering and becoming wealthy. Where Kan Water (坎水) and Xun Water (巽水) converge at the Bright Hall (明堂), a Formation known as the 4-1 In the Same Palace (四一同宮) will be produced; which indicates that at least someone in the family will rise to a high government position, and become famous. Indeed, such a Formation would complete or consummate Early Heaven (先天) and Later Heaven (後天), whereby one's fame, fortune and status will be perpetually ensured.

Incoming Kan Water (坎水來), which combines with Xun 巽 to produce a Formation will also bring about two distinct outcomes. Where a Gen Exit (艮) is seen, the outcomes will be extremely auspicious. Similar outcomes may be expected as well, should a Zhen Exit (震) at Jia 甲 and Yi 乙 be present.

10. Kun Formation

Sitting : **Kun 坤**   Facing : **Gen 艮**

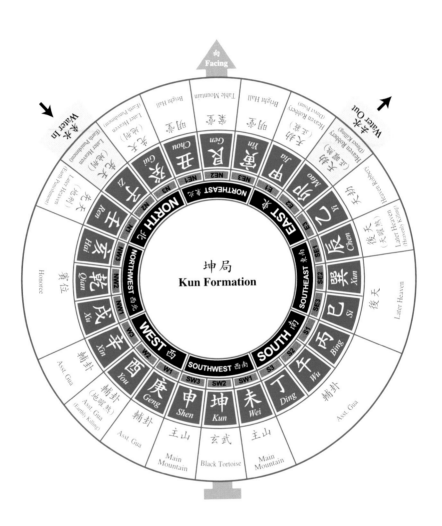

坤局
Kun Formation

10.	Kun Formation		
Water In :	**Zi** 子	Water Out :	**Mao** 卯

However, Incoming Water from Kan, Exiting at Zhen (坎水出震) is 'Rebellious Water'; otherwise known as Counter-Leaping Water (反跳水). Such an occurrence indicates great wealth and relationship luck, although one's children may also tend to behave in a rebellious or disobedient manner.

11.	Kun Formation		
	Sitting :	**Kun** 坤	Facing :	**Gen** 艮

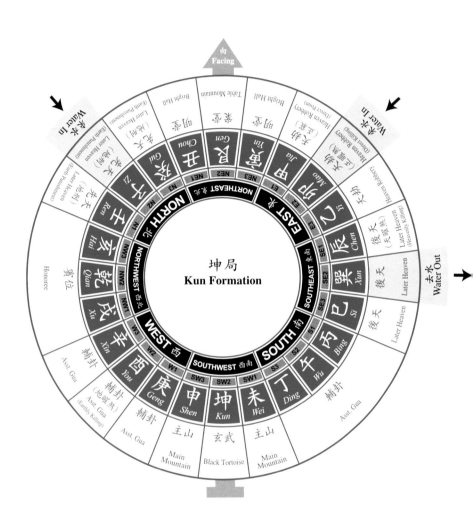

坤局
Kun Formation

11.	Kun Formation

Water In : **Zi** 子, **Mao** 卯   Water Out :   **Xun** 巽

Incoming Zhen Water (震水) meeting with Kan Water (坎水) and flowing out via Xun 巽 is also known as Later Heaven Clash Out (後天流破). This is a generally inauspicious Formation, which indicates that each and every generation of one's descendents will suffer from poverty and loss of wealth, or the possibility of a miscarriage or divorce in the family. Despite one's luck appearing to be initially prosperous, when the Annual Earth Luck (地運流年) (Year Star) reaches the Water Mouth (水口), one may encounter a divorce, or suffer from loss of wealth.

Furthermore, should the Water encounter a Clash Out (流破) in either the Kun 坤 or Dui 兌 Sectors, it would be advisable to either plant a bamboo-plant, or use a rooftop to cover such a Formation.

12. Kun Formation

Sitting : **Kun 坤**   Facing : **Gen 艮**

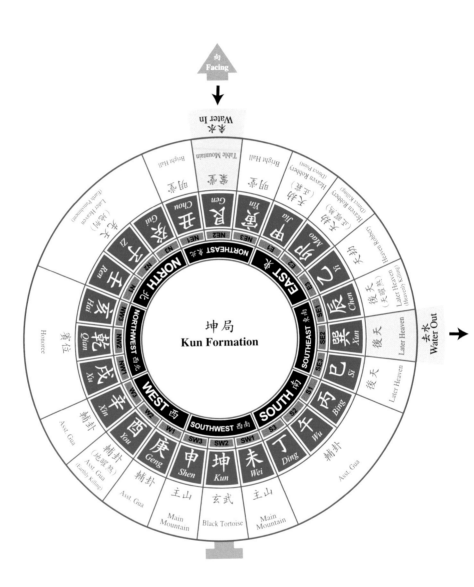

12.	Kun Formation			
	Water In :	**Gen** 艮	Water Out :	**Xun** 巽

The presence of either Water from the Gen Sector (艮水來), or Water to the Xun Sector (巽水來), or the Clashing Out Later Heaven (破後天) could be the harbinger of a sudden death in the family. Where either scenario is seen, one would also need to be mindful of the possibility of a divorce, or family members being involved in prostitution, or adverse outcomes befalling the eldest son.

Water Entering the Chou Sector (丑水流入) is also known as Violent Death Water (惡死水); which means that someone in the family could encounter a fatal accident.

One should also be on the lookout for a road or high-voltage pylon in the Chou 丑 direction, which indicates the possibility of imprisonment.

Similarly, the presence of a T-junction at either Mao 卯 or Chou 丑 is an equally inauspicious harbinger, which indicates suicidal tendencies amongst younger family members.

13. Kun Formation

| Sitting : | **Kun 坤** | Facing : | **Gen 艮** |

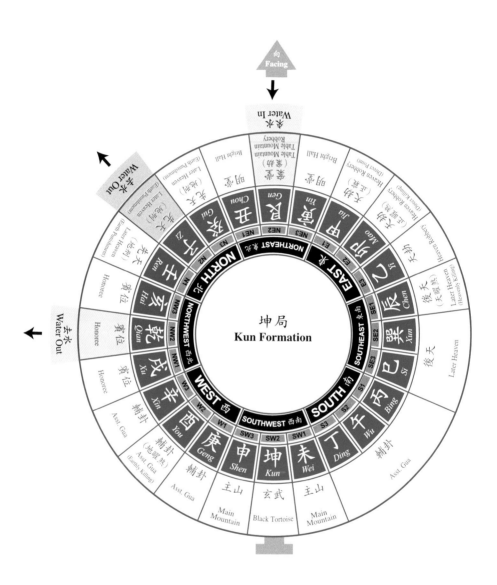

坤局
Kun Formation

13. Kun Formation

Water In : **Gen 艮**   Water Out : **Zi 子，Qian 乾**

Gen Water Flowing Out Qian (艮水來歸乾而去), also known as Incoming Water from Qian, Leaving Gen (乾水來歸艮去), results in what is known as Diminishing Void Total Disaster Water Formation (消亡敗絕水). This is an extremely inauspicious scenario, and where a Formation called Receiving this water to the Bright Hall (收此水過堂) is seen, one may need to be mindful of loneliness and deteriorating luck and fortunes.

Furthermore, the presence of a pit or hole at the Gen 艮 Sector, as well as the presence of a Bright Hall Robbery (堂劫) at Gen 艮, indicates the possibility of blindness affecting someone in the family.

The advent of Gen Water in endangering Kan (艮卦水來囚射坎方) could be the harbinger of a sudden death in the family. Nevertheless, such a Formation could also bring about favorable outcomes to the second son.

In any case, one would need to be mindful where Gen Water (艮水), or Piercing Heart Water (穿心水), is noticed. It is the harbinger of heart attacks, a sudden death in the family, as well as a family member passing away at a relatively young age. Furthermore, the presence of a high-voltage pylon or any such contraption at Gen 艮 is also an indicator of ailments and diseases affecting one's family.

14. Kun Formation

| Sitting : | **Kun** 坤 | Facing : | **Gen** 艮 |

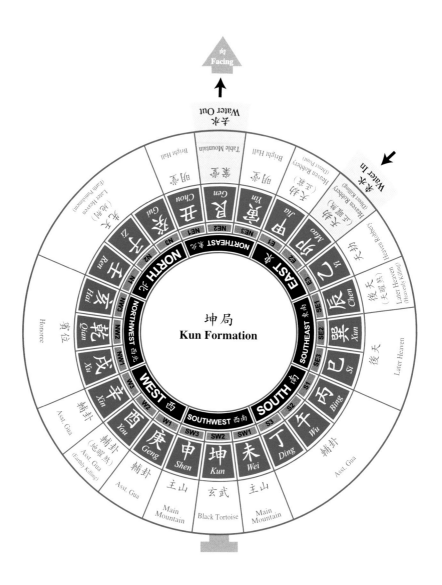

坤局
Kun Formation

14.	Kun Formation		
Water In :	**Mao** 卯	Water Out :	**Gen** 艮

Incoming Zhen Water, Returning to Gen (震水來歸艮而去) is another scenario that one would need to be mindful of, as it indicates destruction and damages. Such a Formation would only bring about loneliness, and declining luck and fortunes.

15. Kun Formation

Sitting : **Kun 坤** Facing : **Gen 艮**

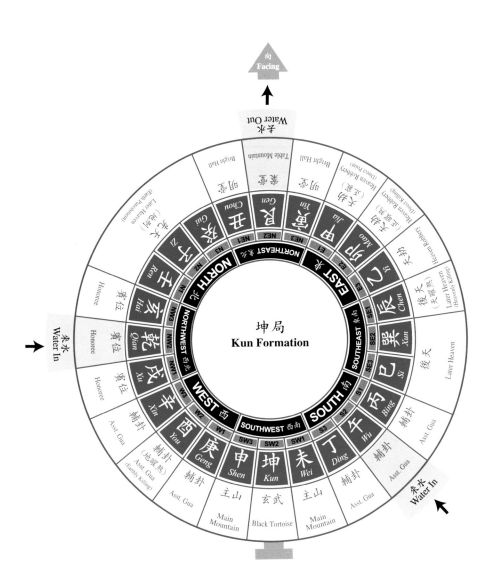

坤局
Kun Formation

15.	Kun Formation		
Water In :	**Wu** 午, **Qian** 乾	Water Out :	**Gen** 艮

Guest Water from Qian and Li Gua passing by the Bright Hall (賓客乾離二卦來) is also known as Guest Water Passing Through the Bright Hall (客水過堂). If this scenario can be matched with both Early Heaven (先天) and Later Heaven (後天), great wealth will be the likely outcome. In addition, one's relationship luck with others will also be favorable and thriving. This is due to the presence of External Benevolent Structure (外益內), which means that the Guest (賓) will assist or aid the Master (主) of the household, to a great extent.

16. Kun Formation

Sitting : **Kun 坤**   Facing : **Gen 艮**

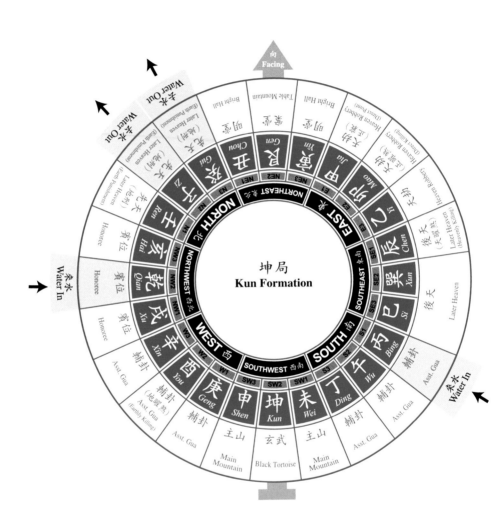

坤局
Kun Formation

16.	Kun Formation		
Water In :	**Bing** 丙 , **Qian** 乾	Water Out :	**Zi** 子 , **Gui** 癸

Guest and Honorary Water converges and leaves through Kan Gua (賓客水收來歸坎而去) is also known as Clashing Out Early Heaven (破先天). It is the harbinger of favorable outcomes for one's daughter's children, although one's son's children will not be privileged to enjoy such luck. In any case, one's son-in-law and daughter's children will be outstanding, and excel in their endeavors.

Similarly, the Formation known as Guest and Honorary Water Shoots through Later Heaven Xun Gua Direction (賓客水來囚射後天巽卦位) will have effects identical to Guest and Honorary Water Converges and Leaves through Kan Gua (賓客水收來歸坎而去).

17. Kun Formation

Sitting :	**Kun** 坤	Facing :	**Gen** 艮

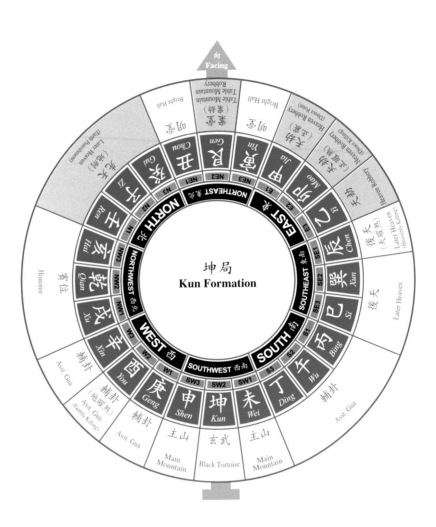

17. Kun Formation

Sitting :   **Kun** 坤   Facing :   **Gen** 艮

One should be mindful of the fact that a Heavenly Robbery Water (天劫水) is an extremely inauspicious form of Water. Indeed, Water that flows from this direction will bring about even more severe or inauspicious outcomes, which include insanity or mental problems, infertility or the inability to bear offspring, as well as bad luck befalling younger family members.

Furthermore, one should also be on the lookout for a rooftop that reaches either the Heavenly Robbery (天劫), Earthly Punishment (地刑) or Hall Robbery Sha (案劫) directions. Such a scenario could result in extremely ominous or inauspicious outcomes, including someone in the family passing away at a relatively young age, and the children in the family being particularly susceptible to injuries.

18. Kun Formation

| Sitting : | **Kun 坤** | Facing : | **Gen 艮** |

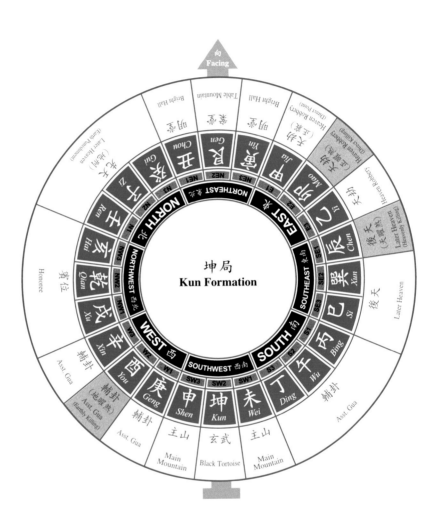

坤局
Kun Formation

18.	Kun Formation			
Sitting :		Kun 坤	Facing :	Gen 艮

The Shimmering Sha (曜煞) direction is also one that must be avoided at all costs, especially if it is facing the main door, an incoming road, or a tall stone wall toward the front of the house. Indeed, where a pile or pillar of rocks, well, handrail, cluster of tress, sharp corner, water-containment tower or chimney points in this direction, poor health and ailments that lead to the coughing up of blood may well follow suit. Furthermore, the presence of any Violates the Shimmering Sha (犯曜煞) or Violates Heavenly Robbery Position (犯天劫位) could indicates the possibility of mental problems and insanity affecting family members.

Similarly, the Formation known as Guest and Honorary Water Shoots through Later Heaven Xun Gua Direction (賓客水收來囚射後天巽卦位) will have identical effects as those pertinent to the Shimmering Sha (曜煞) direction above, should the preceding circumstances take place.

3. Li Formation 離局

1. Li Formation

| Sitting : | **Li** 離 | Facing : | **Kan** 坎 |

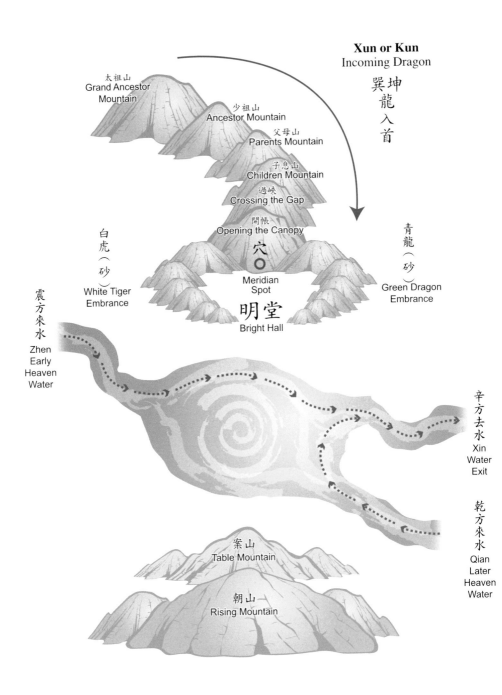

Xun or Kun
Incoming Dragon
巽坤龍入首

太祖山
Grand Ancestor
Mountain

少祖山
Ancestor Mountain

父母山
Parents Mountain

子息山
Children Mountain

過峽
Crossing the Gap

開帳
Opening the Canopy

穴〇
Meridian
Spot

白虎（砂）
White Tiger
Embrance

青龍（砂）
Green Dragon
Embrance

明堂
Bright Hall

震方來水
Zhen
Early
Heaven
Water

辛方去水
Xin
Water
Exit

乾方來水
Qian
Later
Heaven
Water

案山
Table Mountain

朝山
Rising Mountain

1. Li Formation

Sitting : **Li 離**　　　　Facing : **Kan 坎**

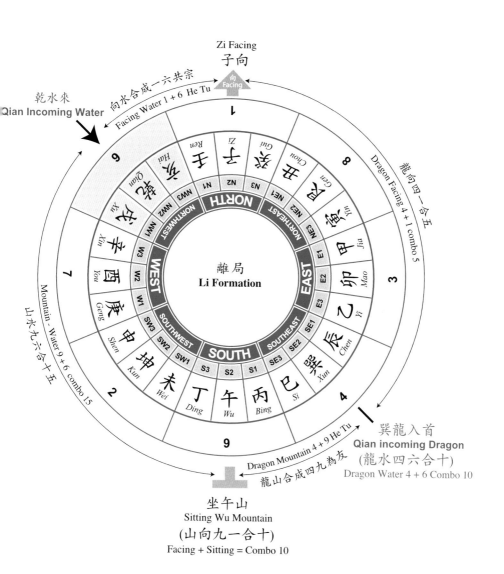

Zi Facing
子向

向水合成一六共宗
Facing Water 1 + 6 He Tu

乾水來
Qian Incoming Water

龍向四一合五
Dragon Facing 4 + 1 combo 5

離局
Li Formation

Mountain - Water 9 + 6 combo 15
山水九六合十五

巽龍入首
Qian incoming Dragon
(龍水四六合十)
Dragon Water 4 + 6 Combo 10

龍山合成四九為友
Dragon Mountain 4 + 9 He Tu

坐午山
Sitting Wu Mountain
(山向九一合十)
Facing + Sitting = Combo 10

1. Li Formation

| Sitting : | Li 離 | Facing : | Kan 坎 |

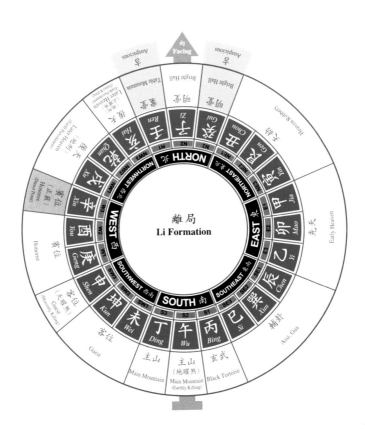

1. Li Formation

Auspicious : **Ren 壬, Gui 癸**

If the Internal Water (內程水) happens to be located at Ren 壬, auspicious outcomes for each and every son in the family may be expected, particularly the second and fourth sons. A Gui Exit (放癸) will also bring about favorable outcomes, although the youngest son will be the first to benefit from such outcomes. Similarly, a Gen Exit (艮) would be most favorable to the eldest son; a Chou Exit (丑) would be most favorable to the second son; while a Hai Exit (亥) would benefit the youngest son the most. It should be noted that Water exiting through any of the Heavenly Stems (天干) is an auspicious sign, and through the Internal Structure (內局), one can predict one's luck cycles over the next 12 years.

The presence of a Direct Position at Xin (政竅在辛), coupled with a significant point of convergence or deep 'container' at Xin 辛 brings about immense wealth and prosperity, as well as outstanding academic and scholarly achievements.

2. Li Formation

Sitting : **Li 離** Facing : **Kan 坎**

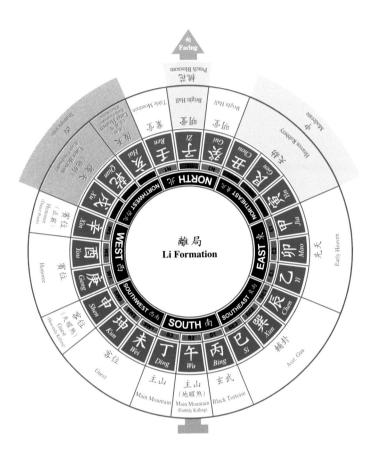

離局
Li Formation

2.	Li Formation				
Inauspicious :	**Xu** 戌 , **Qian** 乾 , **Hai** 亥			Peach Blossom :	**Zi** 子
Moderate :	**Chou** 丑 , **Gen** 艮 , **Yin** 寅				

Internal Water Exit through Qian (內程水放乾) produces what is known as an Internal Structure Clashing Out Later Heaven Formation (內局破後天). This is an inauspicious scenario, which indicates that female family members shall be particularly susceptible to health problems. Where Hai 亥 represents the Shimmering Sha (曜煞) and acts as the Water Mouth during a year with a Punishment (刑) or Solid Field Jupiter (填實歲君), unfortunate outcomes may be expected. Similarly, a Xu Exit (戌) will be most unfavorable to the second son; a Qian Exit (乾) would be most unfavorable to the eldest son, while a Hai Exit (亥) would be most unfavorable to the third son.

An External Structure Gen Exit (外局出艮) will not affect one adversely, although one should be mindful of one's children behaving in a rebellious or disobedient manner. One may also encounter difficulties in siring offspring, and may have to contend with a small family.

3.	Li Formation			
	Sitting :	**Li 離**	Facing :	**Kan 坎**

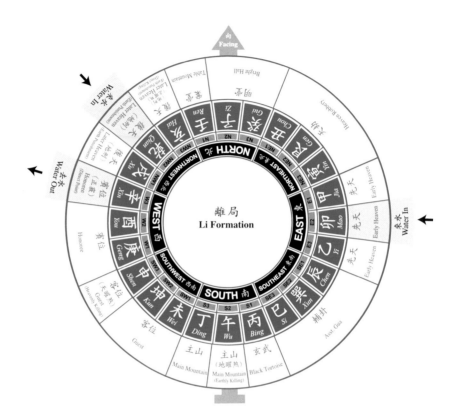

3.	Li Formation			
Water In :	**Qian 乾 , Mao 卯**		Water Out :	**Xin 辛**

Water from the Zhen Position, Passing through the Bright Hall (震水朝來過堂) is an extremely auspicious sign, as it brings about immense wealth and prosperity. Similarly, Water from the Qian Position that Converges, before Flowing Out through the Xin Position (乾水朝來會合後，流出辛位) produces what is known as Obstructed Early and Later Heaven Water Formation 先後天全備, which is the harbinger of wealth and prosperity.

Another auspicious scenario takes place when Water from Zhen Passes through the Hall- Wood Fire Brillance Formation (震水過堂，木火通明). Where such a scenario is seen, one's entire family shall prosper and also become academically acclaimed .

The Direct Position at Xin (正竅位，辛方宜明现) also brings about good luck, although when the Closed Vision Formation (閉目不清) is seen (meaning where water converges but does not exit), there is the possibility of one's family members suffering from poor health, or ailments brought about by weak physical conditions.

4. Li Formation

Sitting : **Li 離**   Facing : **Kan 坎**

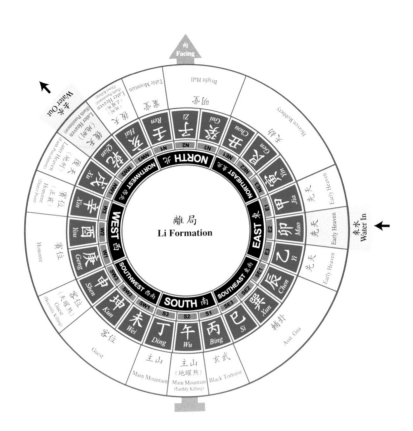

4.	Li Formation		
Water In :	**Mao** 卯	Water Out :	**Qian** 乾

Zhen Water Passing through the Hall, Flowing toward the West and North of Qian Gua (震水過堂，歸西北乾卦而去) is an inauspicious sign, as it is the harbinger of divorce, miscarriage as well as health problems. Meanwhile, a Later Heaven Clash nasty (後天流破) produces what is known as 'rebellious water', whereby each and every generation of one's descendants shall suffer from poverty. This is obviously an inauspicious sign, which brings about what is known as Diminishing Void Total Disaster Formation (消亡敗絕). As one such outcome would be the presence of rebellious children or offspring, it would be advisable to plant a bamboo-plant or cover this scenario with a rooftop, in order to reduce any negative impact.

5. | Li Formation

Sitting : **Li** 離　　　　Facing : **Kan** 坎

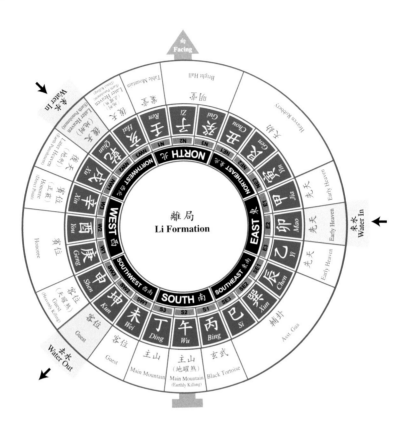

離局
Li Formation

5.	Li Formation			
Water In :	**Qian 乾, Mao 卯**	Water Out :		**Kun 坤**

Zhen Water Passing through the Bright Hall (震水過堂), Converging at Qian (會合乾水), before Flowing Toward Kun (歸坤而去) produces what is known as a complete Early and Later Heaven (先後天) Formation. Where such a Formation is observed, nobility and wealth shall follow suit.

6. Li Formation

Sitting : **Li 離**   Facing : **Kan 坎**

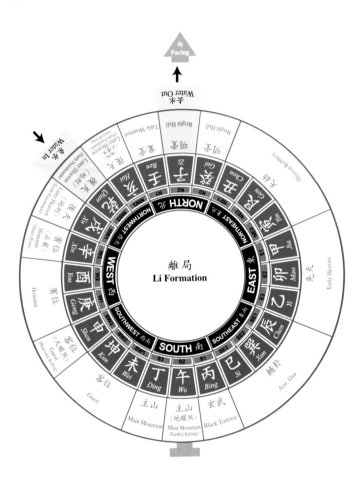

San Yuan Dragon Gate Eight Formations Water Method 三元龍門八局水法

90

6. | Li Formation

Water In : **Qian 乾**   Water Out : **Zi 子**

According to the classical text (劈破前山), the where Water from Qian Gua Exits at Kan (乾卦水來，出坎), the outcomes will be most auspicious and favorable. However, the presence of Heavenly Robbery Water Passing through the Bright Hall (天劫水過堂), which in turn forms a Counter-Bow (反弓), may result in one's children behaving in a rebellious manner, or bring about blood-related ailments, injuries and relationship issues.

7. Li Formation

Sitting : **Li 離**   Facing : **Kan 坎**

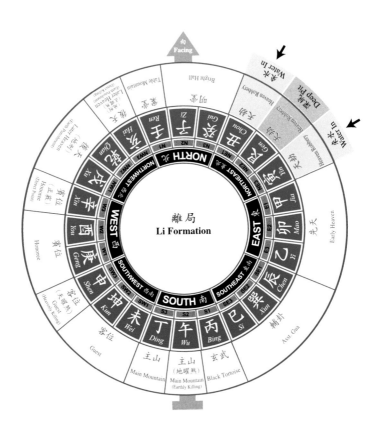

離局
Li Formation

92

7.	Li Formation

Water In : **Chou** 丑, **Yin** 寅   Deep Pit : **Gen** 艮

Water from Chou (丑水來) or the presence of an incoming road from Chou 丑, or T-junction at Chou 丑 is an inauspicious sign, as it is the harbinger of injuries, chronic illnesses and death, including someone committing suicide by hanging him or herself.

The presence of a 'deep pit' or large hole at Gen 艮 indicates the onslaught of eye-related ailments.

Where Water from Yin (寅水來) is seen, there is the possibility of one behaving in a flirtatious or lascivious manner, or worse still, being crushed to death by a large rock or boulder.

8. Li Formation

Sitting : **Li 離**　　　　Facing : **Kan 坎**

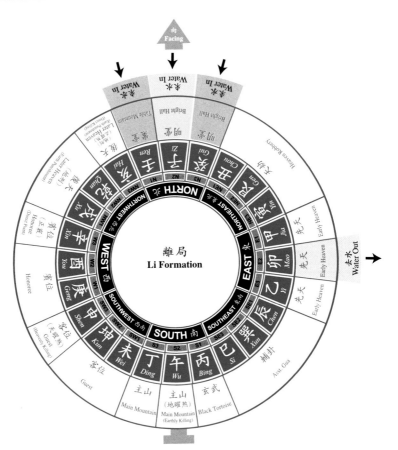

離局
Li Formation

8. Li Formation

Water In : **Ren** 壬 , **Zi** 子 , **Gui** 癸   Water Out :   **Mao** 卯

Bright Hall Robbery Water (堂劫水來), also known as Piercing Heart Water (穿心水), could bring about heart disease or even a sudden death. Meanwhile, Water from Ren (壬水來) indicates the possibility of meeting with a fatal accident. Water from Zi (子水來), also known as E Mei Shui (娥媚水), could lead to female family members behaving in a sexually immoral or lascivious manner. Water from Zi, Flowing toward Mao (子水來，卯水去) is another inauspicious scenario, as it indicates an unhealthy or unreciprocated romance, male family members passing away at a relatively young age, or female family members eloping with their lovers. One should also be mindful where Water from Gui (癸水來) is seen, as it could lead to a death by drowning. This scenario is also known as the Violent Death Water Formation (惡死水) or Poisonous Medicine Water Formation (毒藥水).

Water from Zi or Gui (子癸水來) is the harbinger of numerous health problems, ranging from ailments that lead to internal bleeding, to one being crippled.

Water from Mao, Leaving You (卯水來，酉水去) could mean that one is involved in an unhealthy or immoral romantic relationship.

9. Li Formation

| Sitting : | **Li 離** | Facing : | **Kan 坎** |

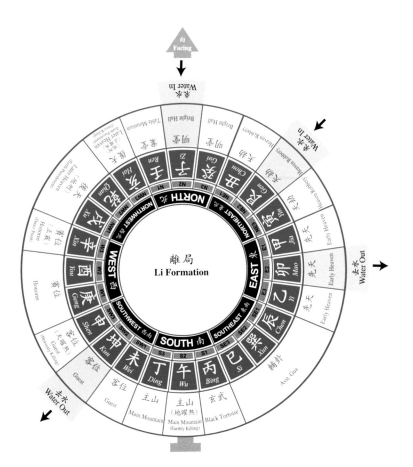

離局
Li Formation

9.	Li Formation		
	Water In : **Zi** 子, **Gen** 艮	Water Out :	**Mao** 卯, **Kun** 坤

Water from Kan (坎水流來), Flowing toward the Kun (坤位去) or Water from Gen (艮水流來), Flowing toward the Zhen (震位去) results in a Diminishing Void Total Disaster Formation (消亡敗絕).

10.	Li Formation			
	Sitting :	**Li 離**	Facing :	**Kan 坎**

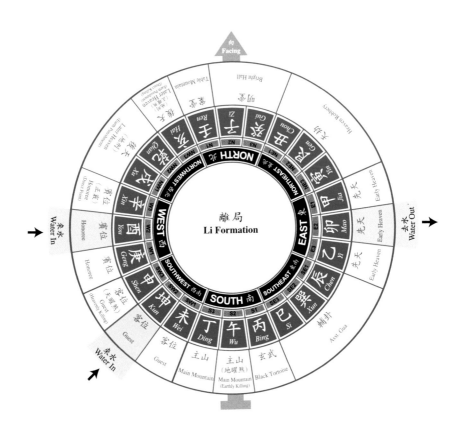

離局
Li Formation

10. Li Formation

Water In : **You** 酉 , **Kun** 坤   Water Out :   **Mao** 卯

The Guest Position Kun and Dui Water that Keeps Flowing through the Bright Hall (賓客坤兌二水收來過堂), before Passing through the Zhen Position (歸震方而去) produces an outcome that Favors the Guest over the Master (倒主蔭客). This indicates that one's daughter's family shall prosper, although the luck of one's son's family shall decline.

11. Li Formation

Sitting : **Li 離** Facing : **Kan 坎**

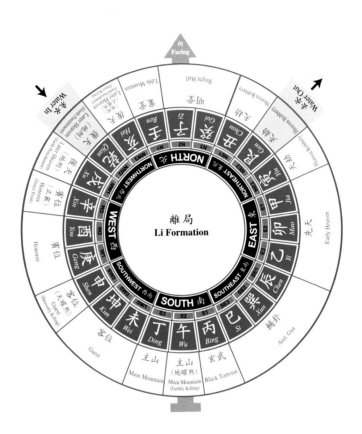

11.	Li Formation			
Water In :	**Qian 乾**		Water Out :	**Gen 艮**

Water from Qian Gua, Exiting through Gen (乾卦水來出艮) produces what is known as 'Rebellious Water' Formation. This is because despite Later Heaven Water Passing by the Hall (後天水過堂), Gen 艮 happens to be located at the edge of Li 離. As such, although one's family may enjoy wealth and good fortune, family and domestic relationships may not be entirely harmonious. Such a scenario is also known as a Diminishing Void Total Disaster Formation (消亡敗絕), whereby the luck of the entire family may eventually decline.

12. Li Formation

Sitting : **Li 離**   Facing : **Kan 坎**

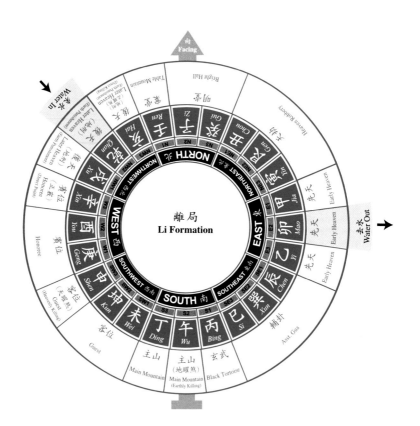

離局
Li Formation

12.	Li Formation		
Water In :	**Qian 乾**	Water Out :	**Mao 卯**

Water from Qian Gua Passing through the Bright Hall, before Flowing toward Zhen (乾卦水過堂，歸震而去) is also known as the Early Heaven Clashing Out Later Heaven Formation (後天破先天). As it also known as the Diminishing Void Total Disaster Formation (消亡敗絕), one's entire family may eventually become disunited and fall apart. The presence of a 'container' or point of convergence at Zhen 震, however, indicates that one's family shall bloom and become larger. Furthermore, wealth and prosperity shall follow suit, as it grows.

13. Li Formation

| Sitting : | **Li 離** | Facing : | **Kan 坎** |

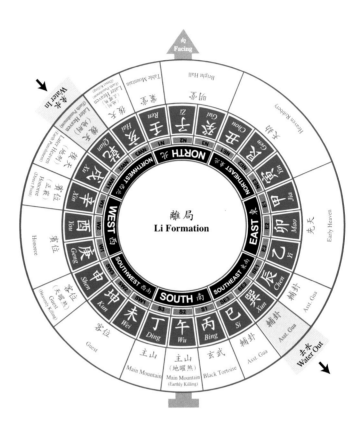

離局
Li Formation

13. Li Formation

| Water In : | Qian 乾 | Water Out : | Xun 巽 |

Water from Later Heaven Qian, Passing through Xun (後天乾水來歸巽而去) brings about wealth and prosperity. Without the presence of Assistants (輔弼), however, one's career path may tend to be challenging and tough. A Hai (亥) Water coming to Bright Hall (亥水朝堂) is also known as Shimmering Sha Water (曜煞水), and where it coincides with a Bright Hall has Robbery Sha (堂前帶劫), mental problems, insanity and kidney ailments could follow suit.

Xu 戌 also represents the position of a 'prison'. As such, the presence of a mountain that resembles a prison, lock or chains, or a winding road that has a robe-like appearance could indicate the possibility of imprisonment. Furthermore, a Sha Qi at the Robbery Direction (劫方殺重) is an extremely ominous indicator of death, while absense of an Elegant Bright Hall (明堂清秀) is the harbinger of legal issues and lawsuits.

Incoming Heavenly Robbery Gen Water, Passes through Bright Hall, exiting at Qian (天劫艮卦水來朝堂，歸乾而去) is another inauspicious scenario, as it indicates the one may suffer from exhaustion, or ailments that lead to the coughing up of blood. Incoming Heavenly Robbery Water (天劫水來) indicates that the eldest son's family shall become disunited and eventually fall apart. Meanwhile, the presence of a Water Clashing Out Later Heaven (流破後天) could result in each and every generation of one's descendents suffering from poverty, while pregnant female family members should be particularly mindful of a miscarriage. There is also the possibility of a nasty divorce. The presence of a 'container' or point of convergence at Qian 乾, however, indicates that a male family member's second marriage will bring him wealth and prosperity, although male family members may tend to behave in a sexually immoral or lascivious manner.

14. Li Formation

| Sitting : | **Li 離** | Facing : | **Kan 坎** |

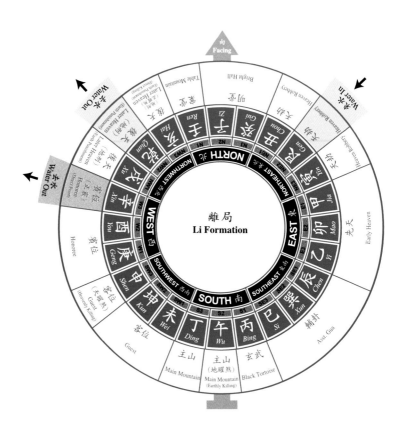

離局
Li Formation

14.	Li Formation
Water In : **Gen** 艮	Water Out : **Qian** 乾, **Xin** 辛

Gen Water Passing through the Bright Hall, before Entering Xin (艮水過堂，入辛) results in what is known as Direct Position (正竅). Where 'Inauspicious Water' Passes through the Bright Hall (過堂), the third son's family may become disunited and eventually fall apart.

15. Li Formation

Sitting : **Li 離**   Facing : **Kan 坎**

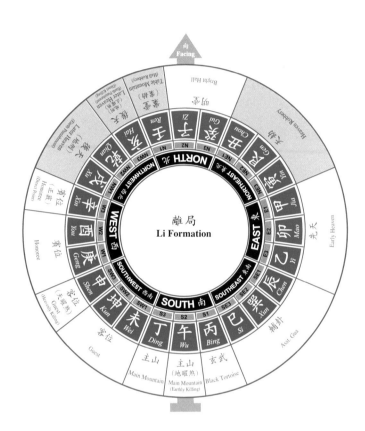

離局
Li Formation

15.	Li Formation			
Sitting :		**Li** 離	Facing :	**Kan** 坎

One should be mindful of the presence of a rooftop or pointed object located at the Heavenly Roberry (天劫), Earthly Punishment (地刑) or Hall Robbery Sha (案劫) position. Similarly, the presence of a pile of rocks, large rock, high-voltage pylon or old well located within 20 meters from the Bright Hall (明堂) is also cause for concern. These features could result in injuries, ailments that lead to the coughing up of blood, exhaustion, harm befalling family members, car accidents or even someone being killed in a robbery.

16.	Li Formation		
Sitting :	**Li 離**	Facing :	**Kan 坎**

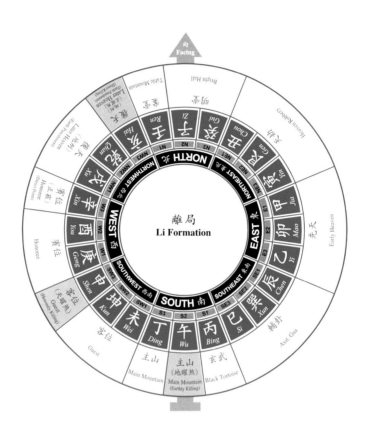

16.	Li Formation			
	Sitting :	Li 離	Facing :	Kan 坎

The presence of a large tree, big rock, pointed rooftop, wall corner or lamppost at Wu 午 is the harbinger of migraines, eye injuries, high blood pressure or hypertension, and illnesses that are not easily detectable. In fact, the presence of a pond at Wu 午 indicates the possibility of blindness, while back injuries may follow suit should Wu 午 happen to be located at the back of one's house. Where Wu 午 represents the 'Prison Star', there is the possibility of one being imprisoned. Should there be a Clashing Road (路沖) at Wu 午, one may incur financial losses arising from relationship issues.

The presence of a temple or place of worship at Shen 申 could result in disharmony and chaos affecting one's family, a divorce, a dispute or even an illness that is not easily detectable. As such, it would be advisable to avoid having the main door, a tree, or incoming water or road at Hai 亥, as such features could lead to headaches, kidney problems and spiritual disturbances.

4. Kan Formation 坎局

1. Kan Formation

Sitting : **Kan 坎**　　　　Facing : **Li 離**

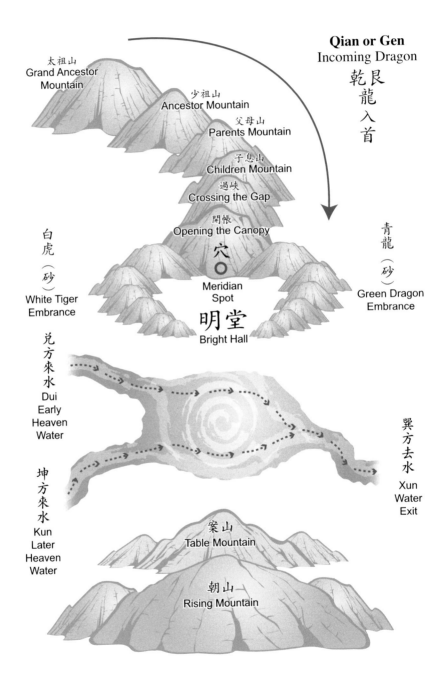

Qian or Gen
Incoming Dragon
乾艮龍入首

太祖山
Grand Ancestor Mountain

少祖山
Ancestor Mountain

父母山
Parents Mountain

子息山
Children Mountain

過峽
Crossing the Gap

開帳
Opening the Canopy

穴
Meridian Spot

白虎
（砂）
White Tiger Embrance

青龍
（砂）
Green Dragon Embrance

明堂
Bright Hall

兌方來水
Dui Early Heaven Water

巽方去水
Xun Water Exit

坤方來水
Kun Later Heaven Water

案山
Table Mountain

朝山
Rising Mountain

1. Kan Formation

Sitting : **Kan 坎**   Facing : **Li 離**

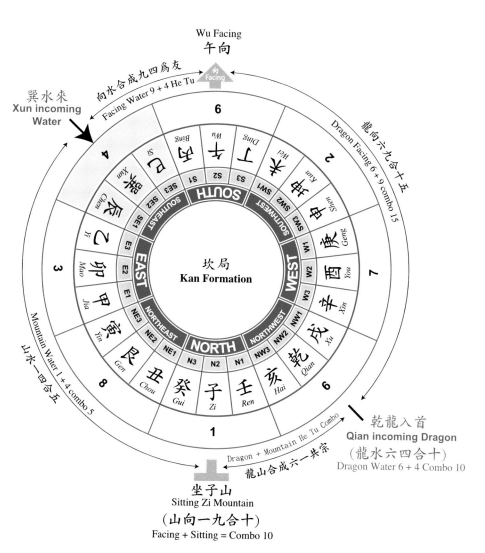

Wu Facing
午向

巽水來
Xun incoming Water

向水合成九四為友
Facing Water 9 + 4 He Tu

龍向六九合十五
Dragon Facing 6 + 9 combo 15

坎局
Kan Formation

Mountain Water 1 + 4 combo 5
山水一四合五

乾龍入首
Qian incoming Dragon
（龍水六四合十）
Dragon Water 6 + 4 Combo 10

Dragon + Mountain He Tu Combo
龍山合成六一共宗

坐子山
Sitting Zi Mountain
（山向一九合十）
Facing + Sitting = Combo 10

115

1. Kan Formation

Sitting : **Kan** 坎   Facing : **Li** 離

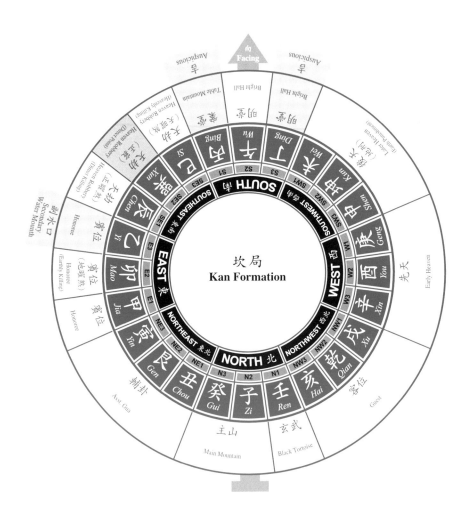

1. Kan Formation

Auspicious : **Bing** 丙 , **Ding** 丁   Secondary Water Mouth :   **Yi** 乙

If the Internal Water (內程水) were to flow toward the Bing 丙 direction, this will bring about favorable outcomes for everyone in the family. However, the eldest and fourth sons may be expected to be the first recipients of such favorable outcomes. Should the Internal Water flow toward the Ding 丁 direction, good outcomes may also be expected, although the youngest son in the family shall reap the maximum benefits from these outcomes.

If the Water flows towards the Xun 巽 direction, the eldest son will prosper accordingly and be wealthy. Meanwhile, one may also expect the grandchildren in the family to possess a fairly high level of intelligence. Such a Formation is also favorable to the third son, although it will prove to be unfavorable to the second son. As the Chen 辰 and Si 巳 directions are only 1° on either side of Xun, however, any errors in the Water Measure (量水) such as Water flowing out from any of the 12 Earthly Branches (地支) directions may result in tragedy. In particular, a killing Qi in the Shimmering Sha (曜煞) or the consequence of a Grand Duke, (太歲刑沖填實) could well lead to an unfortunate outcome. Water should not enter from the Heavenly Robbery sector (天劫) at all times.

Should one use the Yi 乙 direction as the Water Mouth (水口), this could result in ushering of wealth and nobility Qi, which could also see the third son prospering accordingly. However, the luck of the eldest son would only be average, at best, while the second son will find the outcomes of this Formation to be unfavorable.

2. Kan Formation

| Sitting : | **Kan** 坎 | Facing : | **Li** 離 |

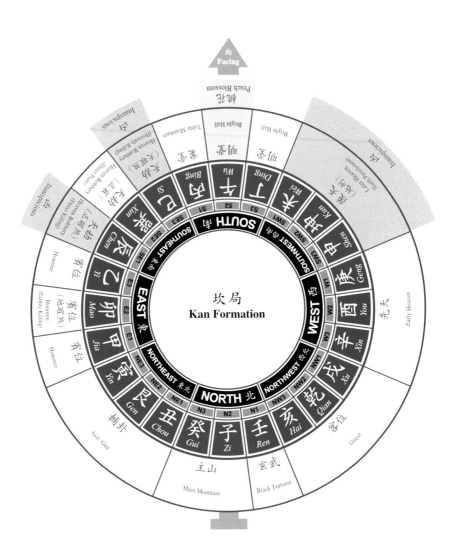

坎局
Kan Formation

2.	Kan Formation		
Inauspicious :	**Chen** 辰 **, Si** 巳 **, Wei** 未 **, Kun** 坤 **, Shen** 申	Peach Blossom :	**Wu** 午

The Water Return to Kun Gua (水歸坤卦) is also known as the Later Heaven position (後天位). It is usually the harbinger of a great failure or lack of success when water exits from this direction. In particular, where the "Clash Out of Later Heaven (流破後天)" is seen, ladies are advised to be mindful of their health. A Wei (未) Exit will result in unfavorable outcomes for the second son, a Kun (坤) Exit will produce unfavorable outcomes for the eldest son, while a Shen (申) Exit will be unfavorable to the youngest son in the family. Furthermore, any of the preceding Formations could also cause ladies to suffer from hormonal imbalance problems or other such related ailments.

A Chen (辰) Exit will produce favorable outcomes for the eldest and second sons. During Dragon (*Chen* 辰) and Xu (*Dog* 戌) years, however, such favorable outcomes could manifest in the form of good financial and wealth luck, although they may well prove to be unfavorable to other family members. In addition, one should also be mindful of any possible legal entanglements or issues.

During Tiger (*Yin* 寅), Monkey (*Shen* 申), Snake (*Si* 巳) and Pig (*Hai* 亥) years, a Si (巳) Exit may bring about unfavorable outcomes and events affecting one's family members. One should also guard against physical injuries as well as monetary or financial losses.

A Wu (午) Exit may see one being initially blessed with good luck, although relationship problems could be expected, eventually. Ladies, too, need to be mindful of their health. This is because Wu (午) Horse is a Peach Blossom Exit.

If the Water Mouth (水口) is conspicuous or noticeable, one will benefit from excellent wealth and family luck. Look out, however, for the presence of any trees or buildings that block this Water Mouth. Otherwise, this may well lead to the adverse Tapered Sha (閉殺不清)condition, which is the harbinger of ailments, sickness and eye-related problems.

3. Kan Formation

Sitting : **Kan** 坎   Facing : **Li** 離

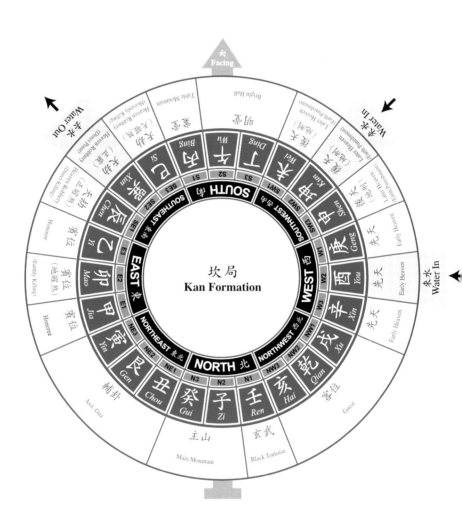

坎局
Kan Formation

3. Kan Formation

Water In : **Kun** 坤 , **You** 酉   Water Out :   **Xun** 巽

Water from Dui Gua, converging with Kun Gua, Exiting through Xun Direction (兌卦水與坤卦水會合歸巽). If the second son is to benefit from this Formation, though, the flow of Water needs to be redirected towards the Li 離 Direction. Should it exit from the Xun 巽 Direction, though, the luck of the second son will be unfavorable. Given the proper Water Formation, though, the entire family shall prosper and become wealthy accordingly. Where the water formation is favorable, this water exit may foster two generations of wealth.

4. Kan Formation

Sitting : **Kan 坎**   Facing : **Li 離**

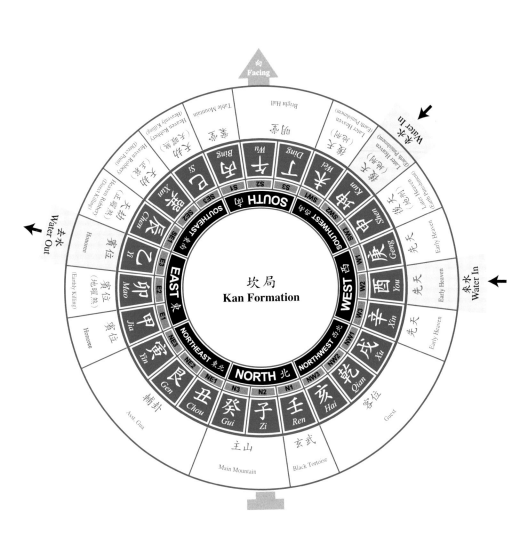

坎局
Kan Formation

4.	Kan Formation

Water In : **Kun 坤 , You 酉**   **Water Out :**   **Yi 乙**

Water from Dui Gua, converging with Kun Gua (兌卦水與坤卦水會合) forms an auspicious Formation, whereby all of one's three sons shall prosper consequently. The third son will benefit the most, with the second son prospering the least. The water is incoming from the Early Heaven, bringing in infinite prosperity and helpful- people luck. The exit of water negates all the negative stagnant Qi from this premises.

5. Kan Formation

Sitting : **Kan 坎**   Facing : **Li 離**

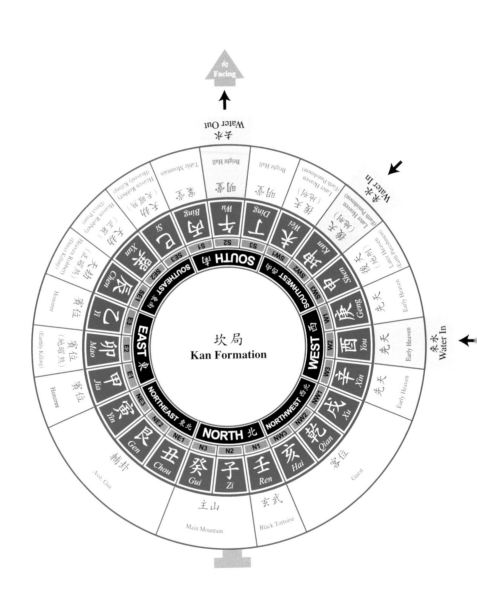

5. Kan Formation

Water In : **Kun 坤 , You 酉**　　　Water Out : **Wu 午**

Water Incoming from Kun Gua (坤卦水來) in this Kan Formation indicates that one will prosper and be wealthy, although lacking in wisdom. However, should Kun Gua Water (坤卦水) combine with Dui Water (兌水) at Li 離, the resultant Formation will produce vast amounts of wealth and bring about great nobility and wisdom to the household.

A Bing (丙) Exit will produce wealthy individuals in the family, as well as allow for assets to be amassed. Meanwhile, a Ding (丁) Exit will prove to be most favorable and beneficial in outcome to the youngest son.

Should a Wu (午) Exit be present, one's initial luck and fortunes may be favorable, although relationship problems may manifest themselves eventually. Ladies need to be mindful of their health, as well.

While water exiting Wu (午) is favorable, water should not be seen to be directly and openly leaving. An embraced exit is vital for the prosperity of this formation.

Kun Gua (坤卦) is also, the Earth Punishment Position (地刑位), while Kun Water (坤水) for this setup is the harbinger of ailments and poor health.

6. Kan Formation

Sitting : **Kan 坎**   Facing : **Li 離**

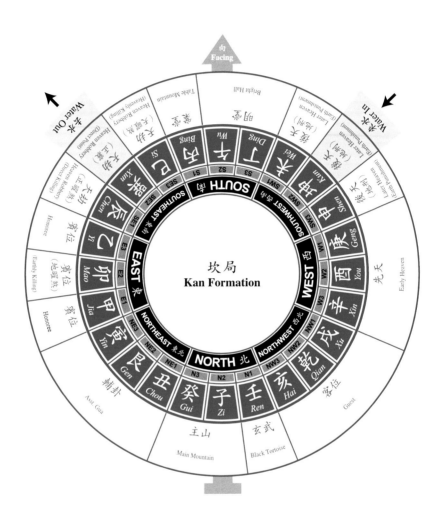

坎局
Kan Formation

6.	Kan Formation

Water In :	**Kun** 坤	Water Out :	**Xun** 巽

Water that flows from the Kun 坤 to the Xun 巽 direction is indeed a good indicator of opulence and great wealth. Unfortunately, there is a trade-off to one's ability to accumulate wealth, as it also forms what is known as Counter Leaping (反跳) Water, which indicates that the male offsprings in the family will tend to be rebellious in nature. If a Xun (巽) Exit is present, the outcomes would be most favorable to the eldest son's children, while being less favorable to the third son, and least favorable to the second son, respectively.

The Direct Position (正竅位) Formation which is the harbinger of ailments and sickness should see water exiting this structure. A Si (巳) Exit will bring about adverse outcomes to the third son. During Pig (Hai 亥) years, the Yin 寅 and Shen 申 Exits will also be unfavorable to one's family members.

The presence of a Chen (辰) Exit, however, will bring about favorable outcomes to the eldest and second sons in the family. In general, they will benefit from excellent wealth luck, although Dragon (Chen 辰) and Dog (Xu 戌) years may turn out to be challenging and tough for those in the family. Such challenges could especially manifest themselves in the form of monetary or financial losses, as well as legal issues and entanglements.

However, where there are regulating mountain stars at the Kun (坤) area, the effects would be first challenging, but eventually extremely positive ending.

7. Kan Formation

Sitting : **Kan 坎**   Facing : **Li 離**

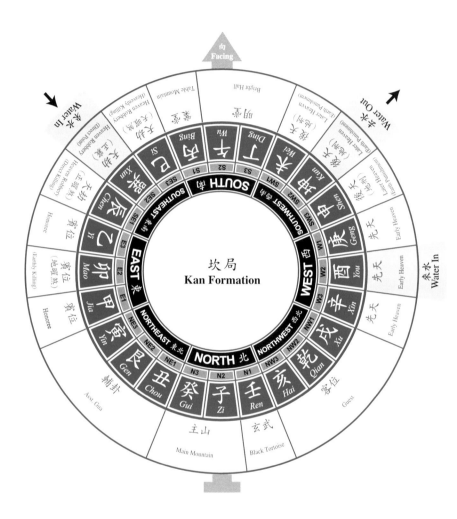

7.	**Kan Formation**		
Water In :	**Xun** 巽 , **You** 酉	Water Out :	**Kun** 坤

When Dui Water (兌水) joins with Xun Water (巽水), [which also represents Heavenly Robbery Water (天劫水)], before moving toward Kun 坤, [which represents the Later Heaven Position (後天位)], the resultant Formation would most likely produce cunning, shrewd but extremely successful individuals. Expectant mothers need to guard against any risks of miscarriage. A Wei (未) Exit would be most unfavorable for the second son; a Kun (坤) Exit would have the similar effect on the eldest son; while a Shen (申) Exit would affect the third son in the family, most adversely.

Under more serious circumstances, these Formations could lead to divorce as well as financial or monetary losses, if the external formation of water is menacing and no Regulating Mountain Stars are present. In addition, Receiving Heavenly Robbery Water (收天劫水) from this direction is an indicator of lung disease, or the possibility of an ailment that could lead to the coughing up of blood.

All these notwithstanding, a conspicuous or large point of collection or convergence such as lake or pond at Kun 坤 would produce immensely wealthy individuals. However, the pool of water needs to be calm and sentimental and water is crystal clear.

8. Kan Formation

| Sitting : | **Kan 坎** | Facing : | **Li 離** |

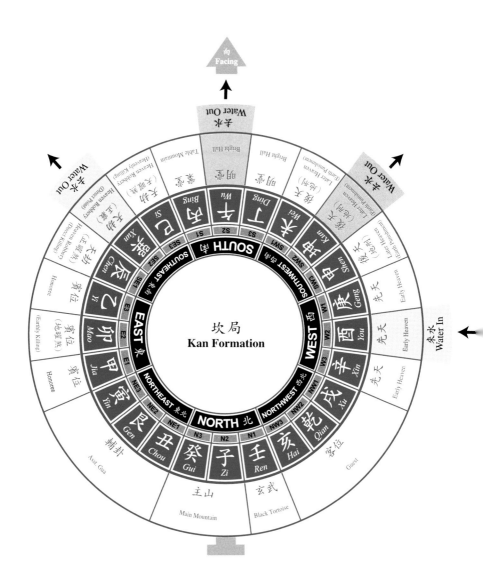

8. Kan Formation

Water In : **You** 酉   Water Out : **Xun** 巽 , **Wu** 午 , **Kun** 坤

Should the Water flow from Dui 兌 and exit through Xun 巽, the eldest son in the family will most likely be blessed with excellent wealth and family luck. However, a Chen (辰) Exit would prove to be most unfavorable to the second son; while a Si (巳) Exit would be most unfavorable to the youngest son. Should either Chen 辰 or Si 巳 be positioned at the Shimmering Sha (曜煞), and meet with a Punishment (刑) or Clash (沖) or, harm (害), from the Grand Duke, bad luck may befall all in the family.

Water that exits through Xun (巽), before turning towards Wu 午 is a possible indicator that the children in the family may possess rebellious dispositions, with other family members afflicted by poor romance luck or prospects. Such water indicates dissipation of wealth. However should the water leave at Xun (巽) and Wu 午, but collects at Xun (巽) in an external water body, all initial failures serve as necessary challenges and learning experience to a highly noble and abundant future.

Should the Water exit through Xun (巽) and then turn toward Kun 坤, the children in the family may turn out to be rebellious, harm may befall one's wife, and there is also the possibility of suffering from financial or monetary losses, as well as a divorce. This is especially true when we have 'Merciless Water' formation like a 'Cutting Feet' sha.

9. | Kan Formation

Sitting : **Kan 坎**   Facing :   **Li 離**

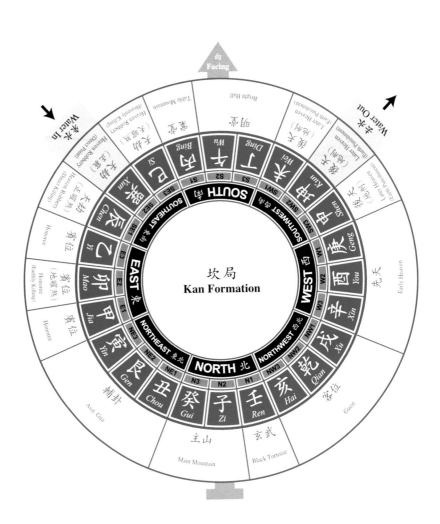

坎局
Kan Formation

9. | Kan Formation

Water In : **Xun 巽**   Water Out : **Kun 坤**

We there is water Incoming from Xun Gua Heavenly Robbery (巽卦天劫水來) present, s a likely indicator that one may encounter challenges and difficulties during one's atter years in life, or in old age.

One would also need to be mindful of a Chen Water Si Robbery (辰水巳劫) or Si Water Chen Robbery (巳水辰劫) Formation, as these could indicate the presence of insane or mentally imbalanced individuals, or unfortunate incidents such as murder, robbery, physical handicaps or injuries, or passing away without leaving a son or heir behind. The Chen Water, Si Robbery (巳水辰劫) Formation pertains to males, while its Si Water, Chen Robbery (巳水辰劫) counterpart pertains to females.

The advent of a Returning to and Leaving from Kun (歸坤而去) is yet another harbinger of a possible divorce, miscarriage or physical injuries. Nevertheless, should there be a large or significant point of convergence such as a river, lake or sea at Kun 坤, one will be privileged to enjoy excellent wealth luck, which will lead to an immense fortune. Indeed, the husband shall be in good stead to prosper accordingly with help from his wife.

The positive or negative aspects of this formation much depends on the quality of the Table Mountain at Li (離) and whether or not the water mouths are locked. If a good Table Mountain and majestic Regulating Water Mouth Stars are present, this formation brings great achievements and abundant good future.

10. Kan Formation

Sitting : **Kan 坎**　　　Facing : **Li 離**

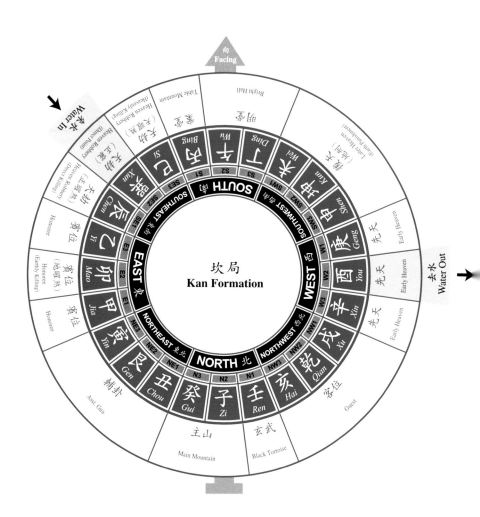

坎局
Kan Formation

10.	Kan Formation			
Water In :	**Xun** 巽		Water Out :	**You** 酉

Whenever Water flows from Xun 巽 in the direction of West Dui (兑), it will form what is known as an External Structure Clashing Out Early Heaven (外局破先天); otherwise also identified as a *Diminishing Void Total Disaster* (消亡敗絕) *Formation*. Under such circumstances, the males in the family will be particularly susceptible to harm and bad fortune, or there may be an ailment that could lead to a coughing up of blood and other lung, throat or respiratory illness. Worse still, one may also be unfortunate enough to pass away at a fairly young age, without leaving a son or heir behind. This Formation is especially unfavorable in outcome to the eldest son. In any case, the involvement of any of the Heavenly Stems (天干) shall affect the males; while any of the Earthly Branches (地支) shall affect the females in the family. One should equally be mindful of a Formation known as Shimmering Sha Water Clashing Out Early Heaven (收曜煞水走破先天), which indicates that one's son could be adopted, or the presence of a threat to one's sanity or peace of mind.

The negative effects would be normal however if the exit water mouth is hidden or unseen.

11. Kan Formation

Sitting : **Kan 坎**   Facing : **Li 離**

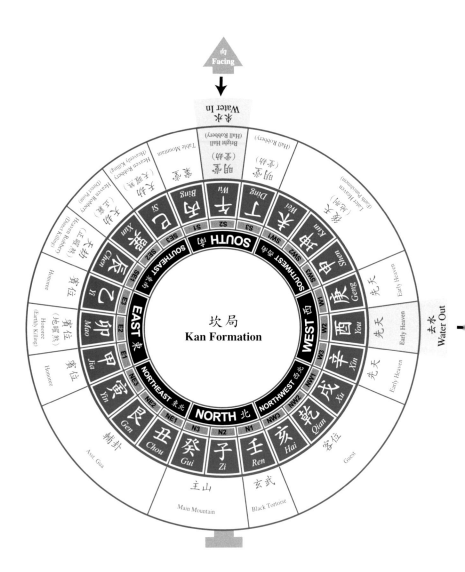

坎局
Kan Formation

11.	Kan Formation		
Water In :	**Wu** 午	Water Out :	**You** 酉

Where Li 離 is at the Bright Hall Robbery (堂劫) position, the incoming Water here produces what is known as Piercing Heart Water (穿心水). As its name ominously implies, this may cause a sudden death in the family. In addition, one needs to guard against acquiring a heart or eye-related ailment.

The advent of a Formation identified as Bing (丙) Road is obstructed by Sha Qi (丙方路來出鬼怪) may means two things: Where the road traveled is long, this refers to the upstairs of a household; where the road traveled is short, this refers to the downstairs of a household.

Should one notice the presence of Water Flowing from Wu, Returning to You (午水來歸酉) or Water Flowing from Wu, Returning to Mao (午水來歸卯), one may need to be mindful of the possible consequences; namely, unstable or turbulent relationships, the males in the family suffering from poor health, the females in the family suffering from a lack of morals or virtues, family members eloping with lovers, or the females in the family afflicted with troubled relationships.

12. Kan Formation

Sitting : **Kan 坎**   Facing : **Li 離**

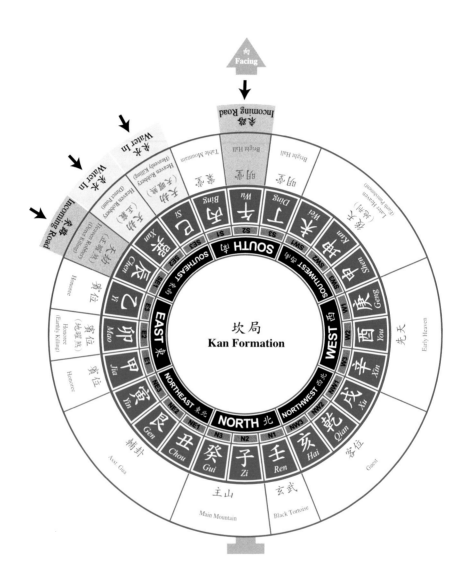

12. | Kan Formation

Water In : **Xun 巽, Si 巳**　　Incoming Road : **Chen 辰, Wu 午**

Water Flowing from the Xun and Si Direction (巽巳方水來) may produce prostitutes or women of loose morals amongst family members. Meanwhile, a Formation known as Road Clashing in from Chen and Wu (辰午方有路沖來) may lead to circumstances where a young male in the family could commit suicide by hanging himself.

This only holds true when the water formation forms an 'Open Legs' water or other Peach Blossom water formations.

13. Kan Formation

Sitting : **Kan 坎**   Facing : **Li 離**

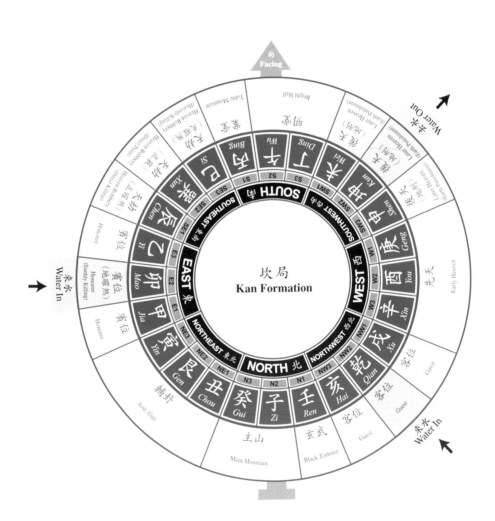

13.	Kan Formation			
	Water In :	**Qian 乾 , Mao 卯**	Water Out :	**Kun 坤**

Water that flows from The Guests' Directions of Zhen and Qian (賓客震乾二方), rapidly toward the Kun 坤 Palace is a most ominous sign, indeed. If anything, it is the harbinger of bad tidings. However, should the flow of Water be contained at the Kun 坤 Palace, one's Guests (賓客) will assist the Master (主) or head of the household to attain great wealth. Then again, while the Master benefits accordingly from his or her Guests, the latter will not enjoy the same level of success or benefits as the former. Furthermore, the women in the family will surpass their male counterparts in terms of success and excellence, while those sitting for examinations shall pass with flying colors.

14. Kan Formation

Sitting : **Kan 坎**   Facing : **Li 離**

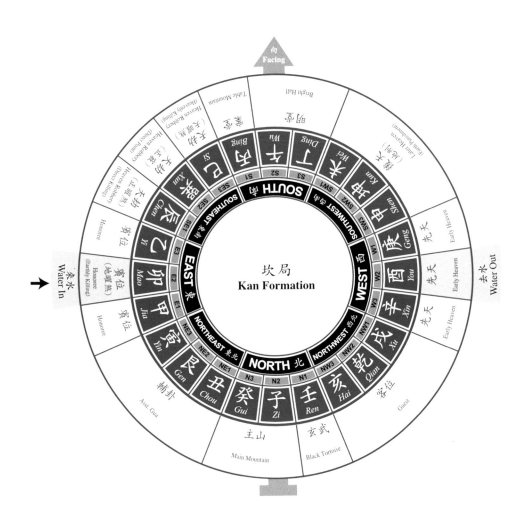

14. Kan Formation

Water In :   **Mao** 卯   Water Out :   **You** 酉

Where Water Flowing from Zhen (震水來), or Water exiting in West (西水去), a Prosper-the-Guest-and-Weaken-the-Master (賓盛主衰) scenario takes place. The effects of such a scenario include one bearing more daughters than sons. Should the Water Pass By the Bright Hall (過堂) on the left side of the house, however, this could be an indicator of a possible divorce in the family. If the Water passes the house on its right side, this indicates the possibility of one having an adopted son, while being afflicted by poor family and wealth luck. In any case, where a Formation known as Exit Water Not Converging (出水無聚) is present, such bad luck may even be worse, with a critical point looming ahead in just a matter of time. If a Geng Exit (庚) is found, the outcomes would affect the second son most adversely; while the outcomes of a You (酉) Exit and Xin (辛) Exit will affect the eldest and third sons, respectively, in an unfavorable manner.

15. Kan Formation

Sitting : **Kan 坎**　　　　　Facing : **Li 離**

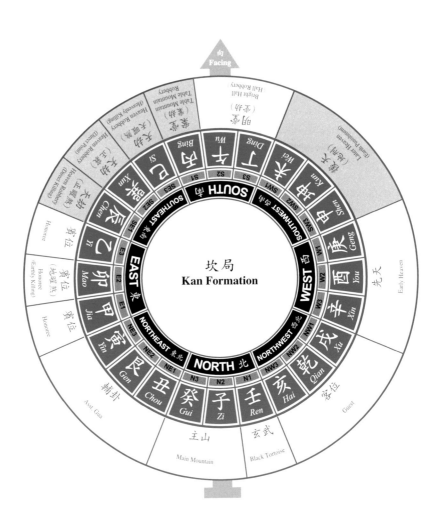

15. Kan Formation

Sitting : **Kan** 坎   Facing :   **Li** 離

Heavenly Robbery (天劫), Hall Robbery Sha (案劫) and Earth Punishment (地刑) form what is known as the Three Knives' Direction (三刀方). Should any of these be found within 10 - 20 meters from the Center of Bright Hall (明堂十字), none of the following objects must be located nearby: An old well, a handrail, a pile of sharp rocks, a sharp corner, a pylon, a fork road, or a pointed item. Furthermore, one needs to guard against encountering an Annual Earth Luck (流年地運) sha, which could result in medical surgeries, car accidents, harm befalling family members, ailments that lead to the coughing up of blood, or any other highly inauspicious event.

16. Kan Formation

Sitting : **Kan 坎**   Facing : **Li 離**

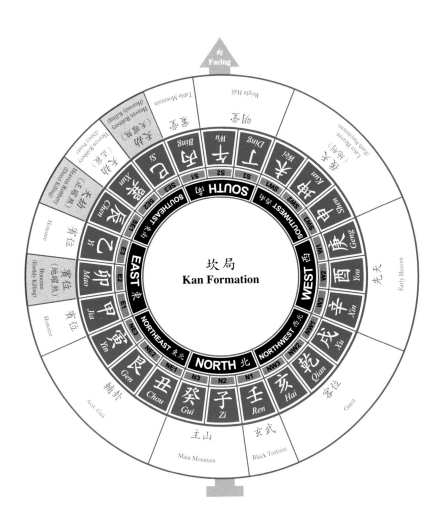

16.	Kan Formation
Sitting :	**Kan** 坎	Facing :	**Li** 離

Should one have a Solid Sitting, and prosperous looking Mountain (坐山豐滿), this is a positive indicator that one's family will prosper and benefit accordingly. Nevertheless, where the embrace is weak, or negative fast moving water, one may suffer from loneliness or lack of companionship in life.

One also needs to be on the lookout for an incoming T-junction at the Wu 午 Palace of the Wei 未, Si 巳 or Mao 卯, or Chen 辰 or Xu 戌 directions. Such scenarios would only lead to a tough or challenging life in one's old age, or could also indicate the risk of imprisonment, legal issues and being troubled by malicious rumors.

5. Zhen Formation 震局

1. Zhen Formation

Sitting : **Zhen 震**   Facing : **Dui 兌**

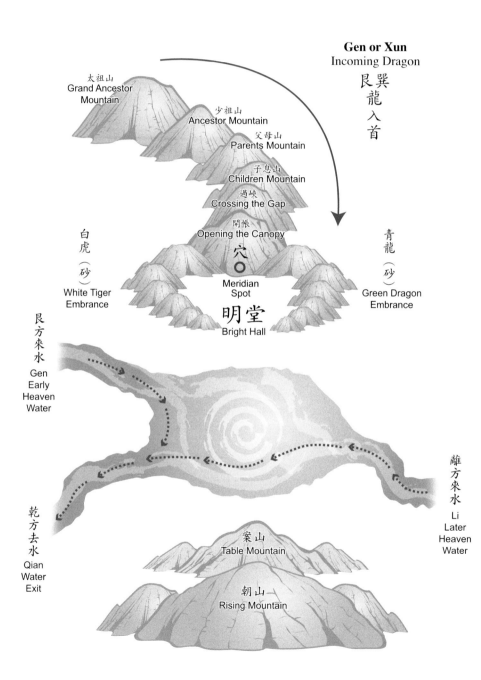

Gen or Xun
Incoming Dragon
艮巽龍入首

太祖山
Grand Ancestor
Mountain

少祖山
Ancestor Mountain

父母山
Parents Mountain

子息山
Children Mountain

過峽
Crossing the Gap

開帳
Opening the Canopy

白虎
（砂）
White Tiger
Embrace

穴
○
Meridian
Spot

明堂
Bright Hall

青龍
（砂）
Green Dragon
Embrace

艮方來水
Gen
Early
Heaven
Water

離方來水
Li
Later
Heaven
Water

乾方去水
Qian
Water
Exit

案山
Table Mountain

朝山
Rising Mountain

San Yuan Dragon Gate Eight Formations Water Method 三元龍門八局水法

1. Zhen Formation

| Sitting : | **Zhen 震** | Facing : | **Dui 兌** |

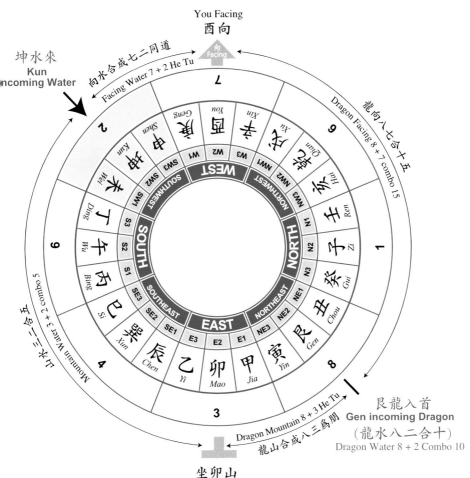

You Facing
酉向

坤水來
Kun
Incoming Water

向水合成七二同道
Facing Water 7 + 2 He Tu

龍向八七合十五
Dragon Facing 8 + 7 combo 15

山水三二合五
Mountain Water 3 + 2 combo 5

艮龍入首
Gen incoming Dragon
（龍水八二合十）
Dragon Water 8 + 2 Combo 10

Dragon Mountain 8 + 3 He Tu
龍山合成八三為朋

坐卯山
Sitting Mao Mountain
（山向三七合十）
Facing + Sitting = Combo 10

1. Zhen Formation

Sitting : **Zhen 震**   Facing : **Dui 兌**

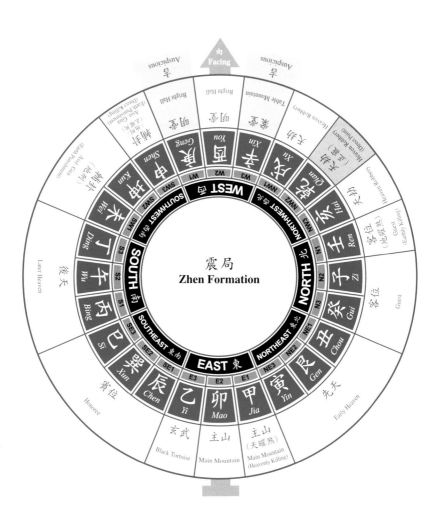

1. Zhen Formation

Auspicious : **Geng 庚, Xin 辛**

If the Internal Water Structure (內局水) are located on the left, then the attributes (family members) of the left side of the property will enjoy the best possible luck from this scenario, and prosper accordingly. Similarly, should the Internal Water Structure (內局水) happen to be located on the right, the attributes (family members) of the right side of the property concerned will benefit accordingly. Where Water flows out from the Central Bright Hall (堂中), good outcomes may be expected, although the second son in the family shall reap the maximum benefits from these outcomes.

Should the External Water Structure (外局水) happen to be found at the Central Hall (堂中), and flow out directly from there, a scenario known as the Dissipating Source Qi (洩盡元神) shall take place, whereupon the luck of everyone in the family, especially that of the second son, shall decline and deteriorate.

Water Flowing toward Qian, Exiting at Direct Point (水流乾位正竅出口) will bring about favorable outcomes to the second and eldest sons in the family, as Xu 戌 shall be protected by Qian 乾. The eldest son, in particular, shall enjoy good wealth luck, although other family members may not be privileged enough to enjoy the same magnitude of this luck. However, the outcomes may prove to be unfavorable to the third son, as Hai 亥 happens to bring about Shimmering Sha (曜煞). In any case, both Geng 庚 and Xin 辛 Mouths shall bring about auspicious, beneficial outcomes to all family members.

2. Zhen Formation

Sitting : **Zhen 震**　　　Facing : **Dui 兌**

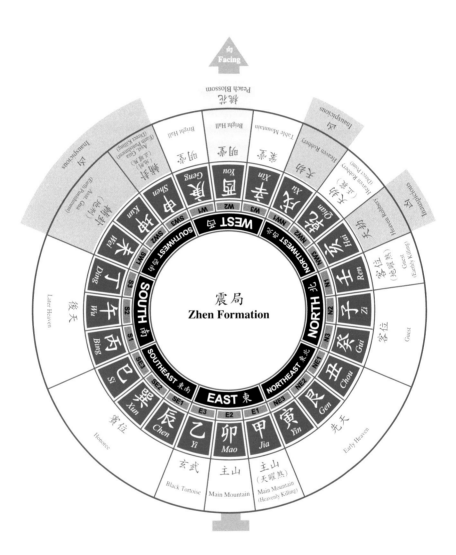

2.	Zhen Formation			
Inauspicious :	**Wei** 未, **Kun** 坤, **Shen** 申, **Xu** 戌, **Hai** 亥		Peach Blossom :	**You** 酉

Kun Water Clashing Earth Punishment (水放坤卦破地刑) is also known as the Assistant Gua Position (輔卦位). It indicates that female family members may be plagued by health problems, as the Noble Star fails to exert its influence here. Where a Wei Exit (未) is seen, the outcomes would be most unfavorable to the second son, while a Kun Exit (坤) would bring about adverse outcomes to the eldest son. Likewise, a Shen Exit (申) would be detrimental to the youngest and eldest sons, as Shen 申 also represents Direct Shimmering (正曜), which is even more consequentially inauspicious.

Meanwhile, a You Exit (酉) brings about Peach Blossom Luck. This means that the presence of a Xu Exit (戌) will also bring the second son good luck at the initial stages of an endeavor. However, such a scenario may not hold true during Dragon (Chen 辰), Pig (Hai 亥), Rabbit (Mao 卯) and Goat (Wei 未) years, where members of the second son's family may be afflicted by bad luck, and susceptible to harm.

Hai 亥 is also a Shimmering Sha position (曜煞位), which means that Water must neither enter not exit from this position; otherwise harm may befall the third son in the family.

3. Zhen Formation

Sitting : **Zhen 震**　　　Facing : **Dui 兌**

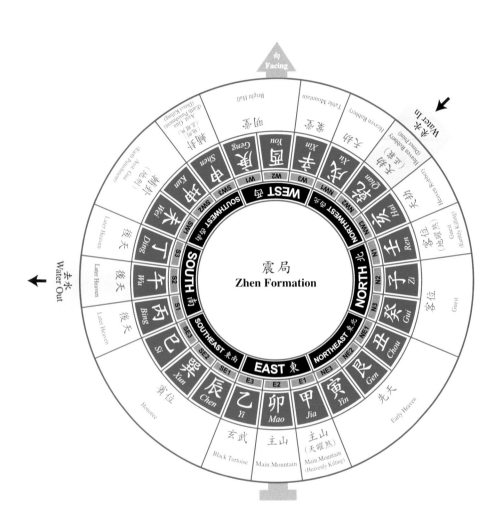

震局
Zhen Formation

3.	Zhen Formation			
Water In :	**Qian 乾**		Water Out :	**Wu 午**

Incoming Water from Qian and Hai, passing through Li (乾亥水來歸離而去) indicates the possibility of family members indulging in adultery or even prostitution. Furthermore, the presence of a tree, Attached with Robbery Sha (帶劫) or something sharp pointing toward the Water Path (水路) at Shen 申 would compound the possibility of something extremely inauspicious taking place. Such a scenario might even result in someone in the family being afflicted with mental problems, or insanity.

The presence of a Clash Out Later Heaven Formation (流破後天) is an equally ominous sign, which indicates the possibility of a divorce, miscarriage as well as each and every generation of one's descendants suffering from poverty and financial difficulties.

4. Zhen Formation

Sitting : **Zhen 震**   Facing : **Dui 兌**

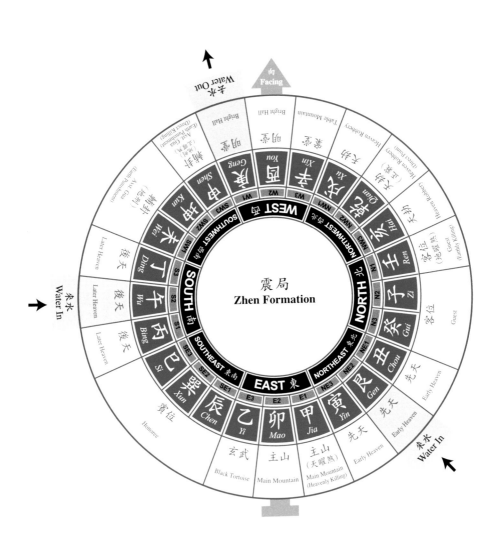

震局
Zhen Formation

4.	**Zhen Formation**			
Water In :	**Gen 艮, Wu 午**	Water Out :		**Geng 庚**

Water from Li, Converging with Gen Water, and Passing through the Geng Direction (離水來會合艮水，歸庚方而去) is an auspicious indication that one's family members will prosper accordingly. It is also known as Receiving Early and Later Heaven Water, Exiting Source (Yuan Shen) Water (收先後天水、出元神水).

5. Zhen Formation

Sitting : **Zhen 震**   Facing : **Dui 兌**

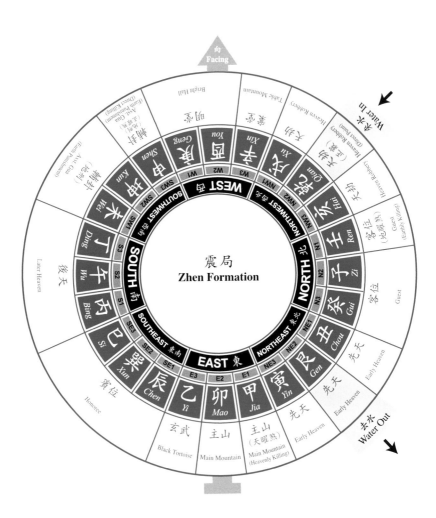

震局
Zhen Formation

5. Zhen Formation

Water In : **Qian 乾**   Water Out : **Gen 艮**

Water Flowing from Qian, Following the Direction of Gen (乾水流來，由艮方而去) forms what is also known as a Diminishing Void Total Disaster (消亡敗絕) Formation. Such a scenario indicates that one may pass away, without leaving a son or heir.

Heavenly Robbery Water from the Qian Direction (乾方天劫水來) is another ominous sign, which indicates the possibility of one suffering from an ailment that could lead to the coughing up of blood. Furthermore, Water Flowing and Passing Through the Gen Direction (水流艮方而去) is an indicator that one may sire many children, although the latter may tragically pass away at a young age.

The presence of a T-junction or incoming Water Path (水路) at Xu 戌 is an extremely inauspicious sign, which is means that someone in the family could be a murder or robbery victim, killed in a war or fight, or face imprisonment. It could also harbor the possibility of a male family member hanging himself to death. Where Hai 亥 is seen, this means a female family members suffering from a similar consequence.

6. Zhen Formation

Sitting : **Zhen 震**   Facing : **Dui 兌**

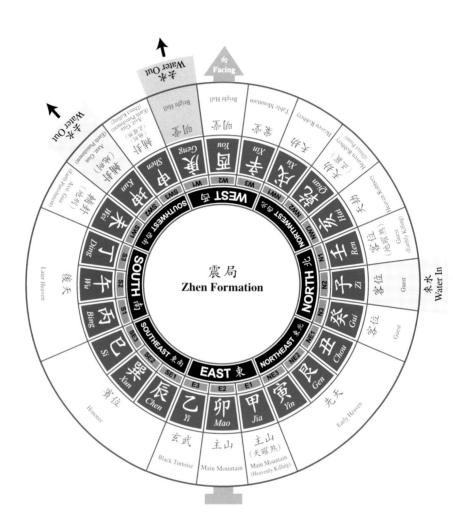

6.	Zhen Formation		
	Water In : **Zi** 子	Water Out :	**Kun** 坤，**Geng** 庚

Incoming Water from Kan, Leaving Kun also forms a Diminishing Void Total Disaster Formation (消亡敗絕), which means that one may pass away without leaving a son or heir.

However, where Water Exits Through the Geng Direction (水出庚方), each and every family member shall prosper accordingly. One should, in any case, be mindful of Water Exiting Through the You Direction (水出酉方), which is the harbinger of relationship problems.

7. Zhen Formation

| Sitting : | **Zhen 震** | Facing : | **Dui 兌** |

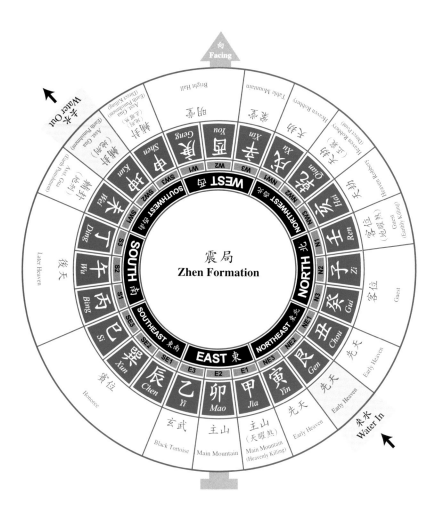

7.	Zhen Formation			
	Water In :	**Gen** 艮	Water Out :	**Kun** 坤

Water Flowing from Gen Passing through the Bright Hall, Countering Out the Kun Direction (艮水來過堂，反跳坤方去) indicates that one's initial luck may appear to be prosperous, although it will eventually decline. The wealth that one amasses will disappear just as quickly as it is earned, and nothing gained is truly permanent. This is because Kun 坤 represents an Earthly Punishment (地刑), which is also an Assistant Gua (輔卦).

8. Zhen Formation

Sitting : **Zhen 震** Facing : **Dui 兌**

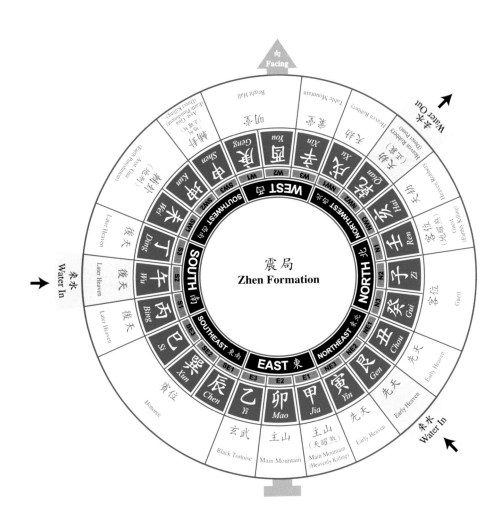

震局
Zhen Formation

8.	Zhen Formation			
Water In :	**Gen** 艮, **Wu** 午	Water Out :		**Qian** 乾

Later Heaven Water from Li, Passing through the Bright Hall (後天離卦水來過堂) denotes the presence of wealthy, although not necessarily intelligent people. Water from Li, Exiting at Qian Gua (離水來出乾卦而去) is also known as the Water Flowing Out Direct Position (水流正竅), which produces noble and wealthy individuals.

Water from Li Converging at Gen Water, Exiting in the Dui Direction (離水來會合 艮水，出兌方), and then flows northwest makes for an excellent Feng Shui location. Those who tap into such a Formation will enjoy both wealth and fame. Indeed, this is the most prominent Water Mouth, where the females in the family will turn out to be pretty and intelligent, while the males will be correspondingly handsome and brilliant.

9. Zhen Formation

Sitting : **Zhen 震**   Facing : **Dui 兌**

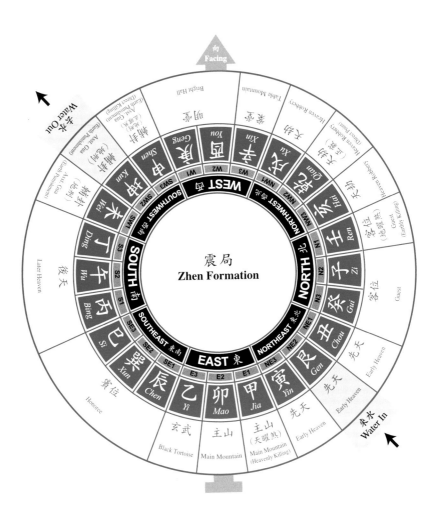

9. Zhen Formation

Water In : **Gen 艮**   Water Out : **Kun 坤**

Early Heaven Water from Gen, Passing through the Bright Hall (先天艮水來過堂) produces wealthy and intelligent individuals. However, Water from Gen, Exiting at Kun (艮水來出坤) is known as a Seaming Flight (斜飛), which is the harbinger of poor health afflicting female family members. Furthermore, other family members will find themselves highly educated, with all the necessary qualifications, but always financially troubled.

Kun 坤 also represents Assistant Gua Position (輔卦位). Hence, should there be a Clash Out toward the Kun Direction (流破坤方) water course, one's career development prospects could be adversely affected. The presence of a Wei Exit (出未) would bring about unfavorable outcomes for the second son; a Kun Exit (出坤) would be detrimental to the eldest son; while a Shen Exit (出申) would be most unfavorable to the third son.

10. Zhen Formation

Sitting : **Zhen 震**　　Facing : **Dui 兌**

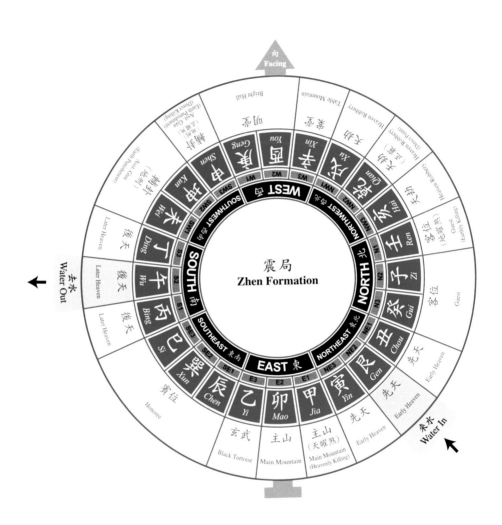

震局
Zhen Formation

10.	Zhen Formation			
Water In :	**Gen** 艮		Water Out :	**Wu** 午

Water from Gen Passing through the Bright Hall (艮水來過堂) also produces wealthy and intelligent individuals. The converse holds true for Incoming Water from Gen, Leaving Li (艮水來離水去), which is also known as Clashing Out Later Heaven Water Formation (破後天). It brings about a nasty divorce and poor wealth luck; in addition to a heightened risk of miscarriage, injury, and every generation of one's descendents suffering from poverty. Where such a scenario is seen, it would be advisable to block the Water Mouth.

11. Zhen Formation

Sitting : **Zhen 震**   Facing : **Dui 兌**

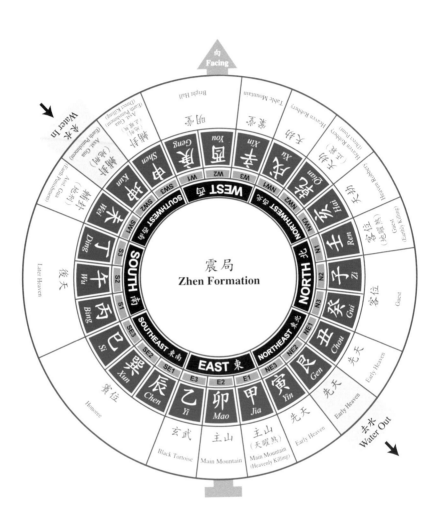

11.	Zhen Formation		
	Water In :	**Kun** 坤	Water Out : **Gen** 艮

Water from Kun Gua, Flowing toward Gen Position (坤卦水來，艮位去) is also known as Water Shooting Through Early Heaven 囚射先天終須絕. This is an ominous formation, which could bring about adverse outcomes to family members that affect the youngest son, in particular.

Furthermore, one would also need to be mindful of Water from the Shen Direction (申方水來), as it poses the risk of someone in the family suffering from mental problems or even insanity.

Where Water Flows from Kun and Shen (坤申水來), the males in the family may tend to be lascivious and behave in a sexually immoral manner. In addition, Seaming Flight Water (斜飛水) is also an indication of loss of wealth and fortune.

12. Zhen Formation

Sitting : **Zhen 震**   Facing : **Dui 兌**

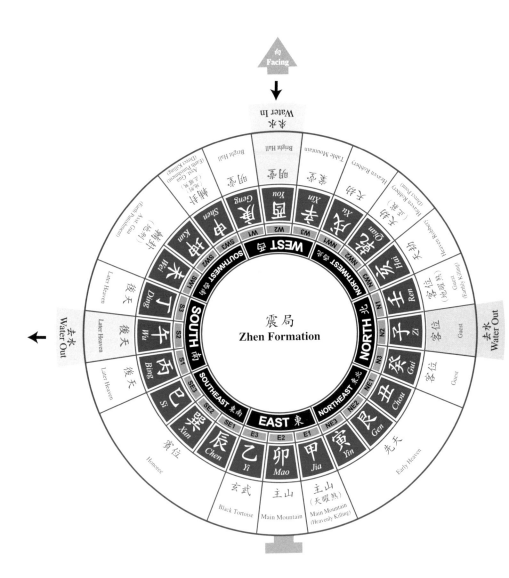

震局
Zhen Formation

12. Zhen Formation

Water In : **You** 酉   Water Out : **Wu** 午, **Zi** 子

Where Dui 兌 happens to be the Bright Hall Robbery (堂劫), Water from the Bright Hall Robbery (堂劫水來) results in Piercing Heart Water (穿心水). This, in turn, may bring about inauspicious outcomes such as ailments that lead to the coughing up of blood, a weak heart, or even a sudden death in the family.

Incoming Water from You, Leaving Wu (酉水來，午水去), otherwise known as Wu Incoming Water, You Exiting Water (午水來酉水來) brings about equally damaging outcomes, especially those affecting relationships. Such consequences include poor Peach Blossom or romance luck, relationship issues and in more serious cases, incest.

Similarly, Water from the Bright Hall Robbery, Passing Through Kan (堂劫水來，歸坎而去) is another ominous sign, which results in a Diminishing Void Total Disaster Formation (消亡敗絕).

The Road from the Geng Direction (庚方路來) is another inauspicious sign, as it indicates that one will encounter challenges and hardship during one's old age.

13. Zhen Formation

Sitting : **Zhen 震**   Facing : **Dui 兌**

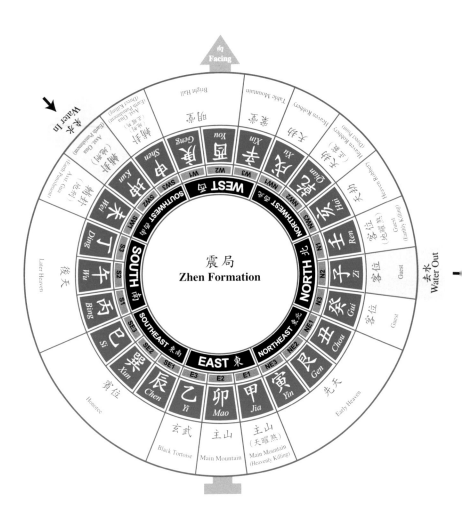

13.	Zhen Formation		
Water In :	**Kun** 坤	Water Out :	**Zi** 子

Incoming Water from Kun, Leaving Kan (坤水來，坎方去) indicates poor wealth luck, whereupon a person will always be struggling financially. This scenario brings about equally unfavorable outcomes for the second son in the family.

Kun 坤 and Shen 申 also form what is known as the Wind Sound Sha (風聲之厄). Where Water flows from either, the males in the family will tend to be lascivious and sexually immoral in behavior. However, one's luck may appear to be good, initially, as Kun 坤 also represents the Assistant Gua Position (輔卦位); an indicator of positive wealth luck.

Meanwhile, Kan 坎 is also known as the Storage Position (庫池位). Where such a Formation is seen, one will eventually encounter failure in one's efforts, despite enjoying a small measure of success in the initial stages.

14. Zhen Formation

Sitting : **Zhen 震**   Facing : **Dui 兌**

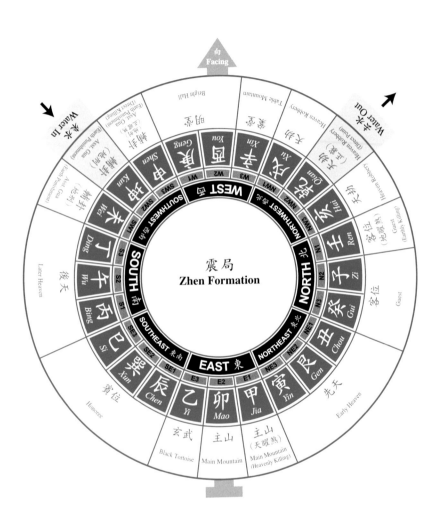

震局
Zhen Formation

14. Zhen Formation

Water In : **Kun 坤**   Water Out : **Qian 乾**

Incoming Water from Kun, Leaving Qian (坤水來，乾方去) is another inauspicious sign. One's children will tend to behave in a rebellious, disobedient manner, while spouses will encounter problems in their relationship with one another. Furthermore, there may also be legal issues to contend with.

If a Reverse-Bow Water (反弓水) is found, the severity of the negative Qi will be doubled.

15. Zhen Formation

Sitting : **Zhen 震**   Facing : **Dui 兌**

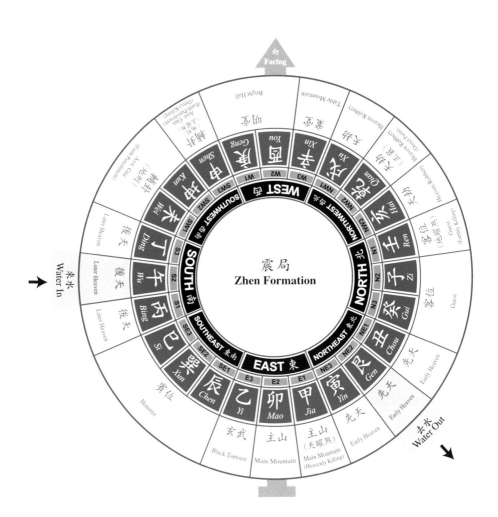

15.	Zhen Formation		
Water In :	**Wu** 午	Water Out :	**Gen** 艮

Water from Later Heaven Li Gua, Passing through the Bright Hall (後天離卦水來過堂), before turning toward the direction of Gen 艮, also forms the Clashing Out Early Heaven Water (破先天). Such a scenario results in a Diminishing Void Total Disaster Formation (消亡敗絕); whereupon one's luck will eventually decline, despite enjoying success in the position initial stages. According to the ancient manuscripts, the Clashing Out of Early Heaven (先天流破終斯絕) brings about, harm to family members, as well as result in a family member passing away at a relatively young age.

16. Zhen Formation

Sitting : **Zhen 震** Facing : **Dui 兌**

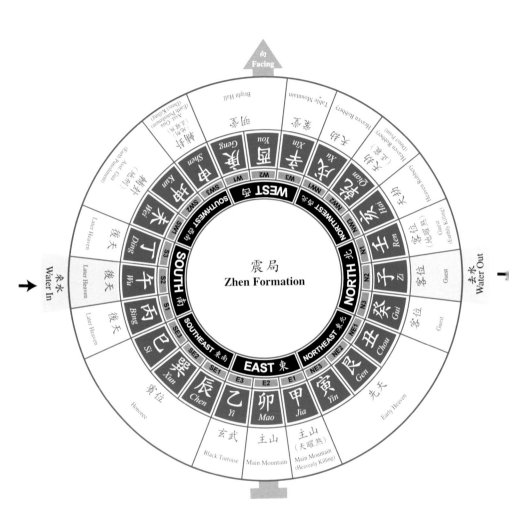

震局
Zhen Formation

16.	Zhen Formation		
Water In :	**Wu** 午	Water Out :	**Zi** 子

Water from Li Gua Passing through the Bright Hall, and Leaving Kan (離卦水來 過堂，歸坎而去) brings about unfavorable outcomes to the second son in the family. However, where a significantly 'deep pool' or point of convergence is seen at Kan 坎, everyone in the family shall prosper accordingly, especially the second son.

17. Zhen Formation

Sitting : **Zhen 震**　　Facing : **Dui 兌**

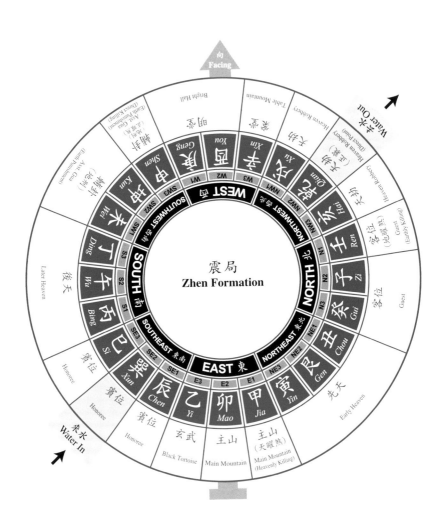

震局
Zhen Formation

17.	Zhen Formation		
	Water In : **Xun 巽**	Water Out :	**Qian 乾**

Incoming Water from Xun, Leaving Qian (巽水來，乾方去) produces the same outcomes as Incoming Water from Kan, Leaving Qian (坎水來，乾方去). These include having more female than male family members, as well as the presence of adopted children in the family. The luck of one's own family members will also decline, although one's sister's family will prosper. Such a scenario could also be described as the Internal Structure Violating External Structure (內益外而敗退).

18. Zhen Formation

Sitting : **Zhen 震**　　　Facing : **Dui 兌**

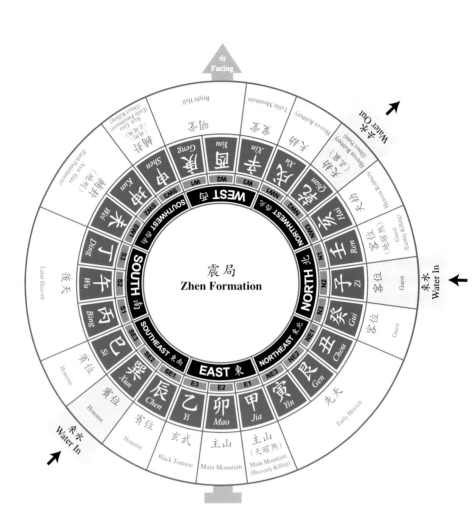

震局
Zhen Formation

18. Zhen Formation

| Water In : | **Zi** 子 , **Xun** 巽 | Water Out : | **Qian** 乾 |

Incoming Water from Xun (巽水來) that flows toward Li Water (離水), converging with Gen Water (艮水) coming from the Kan Direction (坎方), and exiting through the Qian Direction (乾方) is also known as Guest Assisted Early Later Heaven Water Formation (賓客助先後天水). It is an auspicious Formation, indicating that one will sire many children and also prosper in life. Similarly, the Guest Water Assisted Structure (賓客助主) Formation is another auspicious one; also known as External Supporting Internal (外益內).

19. Zhen Formation

Sitting : **Zhen 震**   Facing : **Dui 兑**

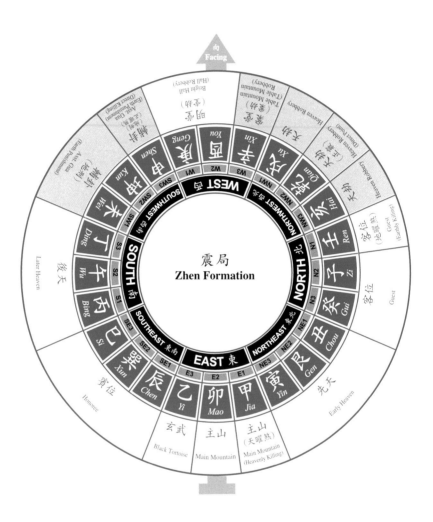

震局
Zhen Formation

19.	Zhen Formation		
Sitting :	**Zhen** 震	Facing :	**Dui** 兌

The risk of injury, harm befalling one's family members, being afflicted with an ailment that leads to the coughing up of blood or the incidence of a robbery or murder is a possibility, should one notice a rooftop or sharp object pointing toward the Heaven Robbery (天劫), Earthly Punishment (地刑) or Hall Robbery Sha (案劫) directions. Such inauspicious outcomes could also take place, where there is a pile of rocks, roundabout, tree, boulder, high-voltage pylon or old well located within close range from the Bright Hall (明堂).

20. Zhen Formation

| Sitting : | **Zhen 震** | Facing : | **Dui 兌** |

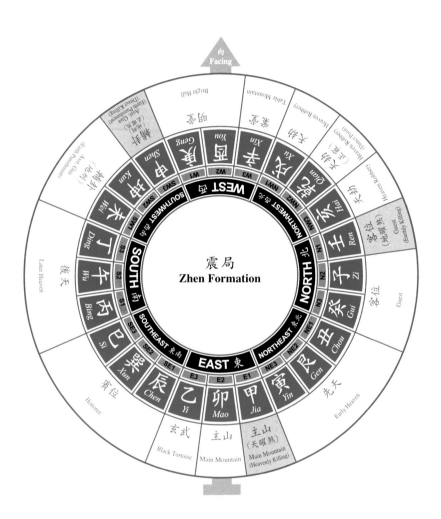

震局
Zhen Formation

190

20.	Zhen Formation		
Sitting :	**Zhen** 震	Facing :	**Dui** 兌

Similarly, the presence of a tree, boulder, sharp roof corner, wall, lamp post or temple at the Effecting Yin (Tiger) and Shen (Monkey) (寅申方犯之) could bring about relationship problems between husband and wife, illnesses that are not easily detectable, as well as religious extremism. Meanwhile, the presence of such features at the Effecting Hai (Pig) Direction (亥方犯之) is the harbinger of ailments affecting the kidneys.

6. Xun Formation 巽局

1. Xun Formation

Sitting : **Xun 巽**　　　Facing : **Qian 乾**

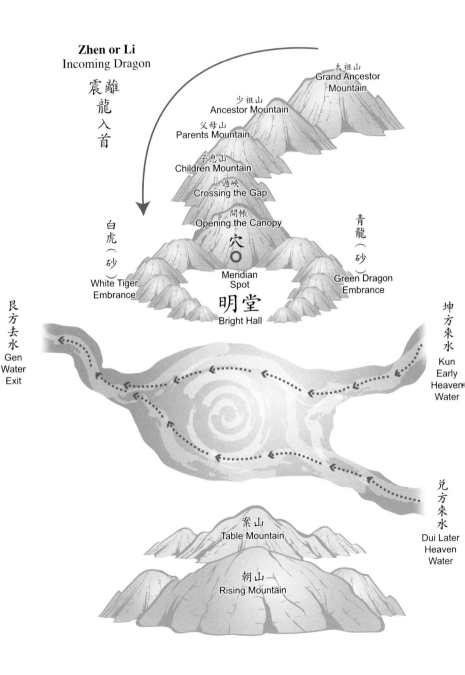

Zhen or Li
Incoming Dragon
震離龍入首

太祖山
Grand Ancestor Mountain

少祖山
Ancestor Mountain

父母山
Parents Mountain

子息山
Children Mountain

過峽
Crossing the Gap

開帳
Opening the Canopy

穴
Meridian Spot

明堂
Bright Hall

白虎（砂）
White Tiger Embrace

青龍（砂）
Green Dragon Embrace

艮方去水
Gen Water Exit

坤方來水
Kun Early Heaven Water

兌方來水
Dui Later Heaven Water

案山
Table Mountain

朝山
Rising Mountain

1. Xun Formation

Sitting :	**Xun 巽**	Facing :	**Qian 乾**

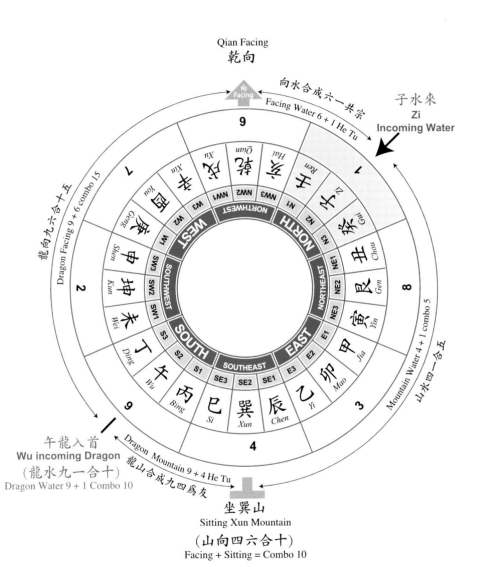

Qian Facing
乾向

向水合成六一共宗
Facing Water 6 + 1 He Tu

子水來
Zi
Incoming Water

龍向九六合十五
Dragon Facing 9 + 6 combo 15

山水四一合五
Mountain Water 4 + 1 combo 5

午龍入首
Wu incoming Dragon
（龍水九一合十）
Dragon Water 9 + 1 Combo 10

龍山合成九四爲友
Dragon Mountain 9 + 4 He Tu

坐巽山
Sitting Xun Mountain
（山向四六合十）
Facing + Sitting = Combo 10

195

1. Xun Formation

| Sitting : | **Xun 巽** | Facing : | **Qian 乾** |

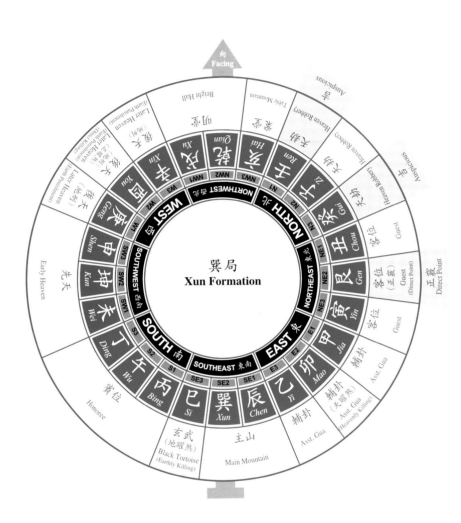

巽局
Xun Formation

Xun Formation

Auspicious : **Ren 壬 , Gui 癸**   Direct Point :   **Gen 艮**

the Internal Water Structure (內局水) is located on the left, then the attributes (family members) of the left side of the property will enjoy the best possible luck from this scenario, and prosper accordingly. Similarly, should the Internal Water Structure (內局水) happen to be located on the right, the attributes (family members) of the right side of the property concerned will benefit accordingly. Where Water flows out from the Central Bright Hall (堂中), favorable outcomes for all family members may be expected, although the second son in the family shall reap the maximum benefits from these outcomes. Meanwhile, the presence of Internal Water (內程水) at Kan Gua (坎卦) would be favorable to the third son, although less so for the eldest son.

Should the External Water Structure (外局水) happen to flow out directly from the Central Bright Hall (堂中), a scenario known as the Dissipating Source Qi Formation (洩盡元神) shall take place, whereupon the luck of the second son, in particular, shall decline and deteriorate.

Central Bright Hall at Qian Gua (堂中乾卦), combined with External Structure Early Heaven (外局先天) and Later Heaven Water passing through the Bright Hall (後天朝水過堂) will, however, produce good-looking and intelligent individuals.

A Ren Exit (出壬) would bring about favorable outcomes to the second son; while a Gui Exit (出癸) would be favorable to the third son, although extremely unfavorable to the second son. It must be noted, however, that even though Gen 艮 represents the Direct Position (正竅位), it cannot be utilized within the Internal Structure (內局). This would bring about an undesirable scenario, known as Internal Structure Exiting through Qian (內局出乾).

As all Water exits are not located on animal signs, there is no need to be concerned of the Grand Duke Star.

2. Xun Formation

Sitting : **Xun 巽**   Facing : **Qian 乾**

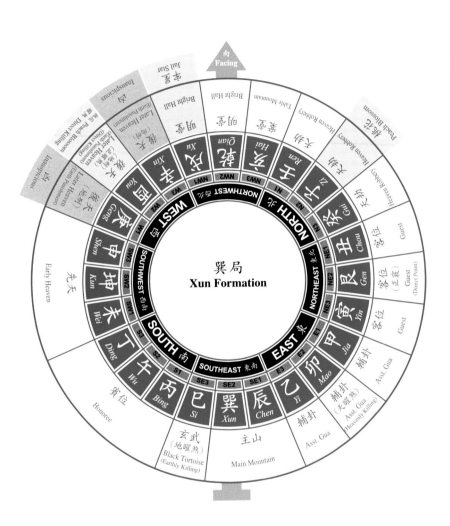

巽局
Xun Formation

2.	Xun Formation		
Inauspicious :	**Geng** 庚，**Xin** 辛	Peach Blossom & Direct Killing :	**You** 酉
Jail Stars :	**Xu** 戌	Peach Blossom :	**Zi** 子

...ternal Structure Water (內局水) and Water Exit from Dui (水放兌宮) combine to ...rm what is known as Later Heaven Position (後天位). It indicates that one will enjoy ...ositive luck during the initial stages of one's endeavors. However, where it meets with ... Punishment Clash (刑沖) or Filling-up Grand Duke (填實歲君), it will bring about ...xtremely inauspicious outcomes; including loss of family members and wealth, poor ...ealth affecting female family members, and a divorce.

...ikewise, the presence of External Structure Water Exit at Dui (外局水放兌), would ...ring about outcomes similar as the preceding case. However, a Geng Exit (庚) would ...e most unfavorable to the second son.

... You Exit (酉) will result in a situation known as Peach Blossom Shimmering Sha (...花兼曜煞), which would affect the eldest son most adversely. One should also be ...indful of a tree or plant blocking the Internal Water (內程水), as this could result in a ...ase of 'split-water', which is the harbinger of eye ailments or worse still, blindness.

199

3. Xun Formation

Sitting : **Xun 巽**   Facing : **Qian 乾**

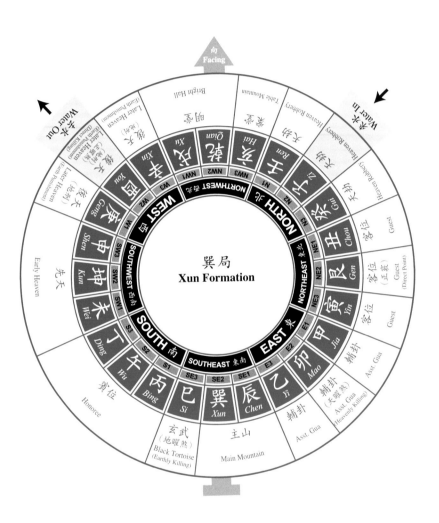

巽局
Xun Formation

3. Xun Formation

Water In :	**Zi** 子	Water Out :	**You** 酉

Where Kan 坎 constitutes a Heavenly Robbery (天劫) of Xun 巽, and Water flows from this Gua 卦, there is a possibility of being afflicted with an ailment that leads to the coughing up of blood and other lung or throat disease. Water from Gui Passing through the Bright Hall (癸水來過堂), also known as the Violent Death Water Formation (惡死水), is another ominous sign, which indicates the possibility of someone drowning to death.

In the event of Water Coming Together from Zi and Gui (子癸同來), one will need to be mindful of chronic illnesses, the danger of drowning, the possibility of a suicide by hanging, as well as health conditions such as piles.

Heavenly Robbery Water, Leaving Dui Water (天劫水來兌水去) indicates the possibility of a miscarriage, dreadful divorce, infidelity or adultery, as well as mental problems or insanity. As it is also considered to be 'rebellious water', one's children may also tend to behave in a disobedient, rebellious manner. Such Water is also known as Wind Sound Water (風聲水).

4. Xun Formation

| Sitting : | **Xun 巽** | Facing : | **Qian 乾** |

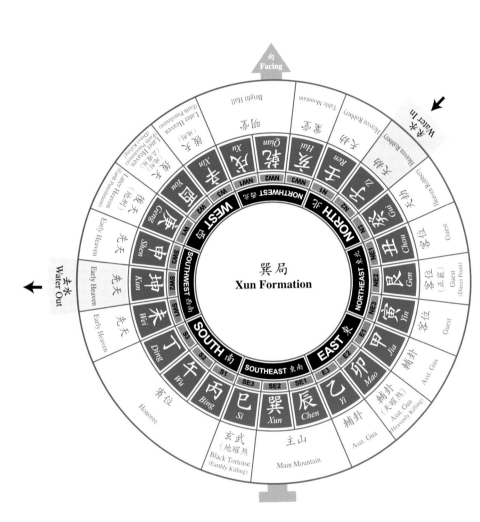

巽局
Xun Formation

4.	Xun Formation			
	Water In :	**Zi** 子	Water Out :	**Kun** 坤

Heavenly Robbery Water from Kan, Leaving Kun Gua (坎卦天劫水來，坤宮去) forms what is known as Clash Out Early Heaven position (走破先天). This is an inauspicious Formation, which indicates that someone in the family may pass away at a relatively young age; as one will sire many children, although perhaps only one son may be left to carry on one's legacy. It is also the harbinger of waning fortunes and declining luck affecting family members.

Where a Kun Exit (坤) is seen, the outcomes will be most unfavorable to the eldest son. Similarly, a Wei Exit (出未) brings about adverse outcomes to the second son, while a Shen Exit (申) would be most unfavorable to the third son.

It is also possible for one to be afflicted with an ailment that leads to the coughing up of blood, lung and throat disease, or even passing away without leaving a son behind. However, should there be a 'container' for Water to converge at Kun 坤, one's family and descendents shall prosper as a result.

The presence of Heavenly Robbery Water Clashing Out Later Heaven at Dui Gua (天劫水破後天兌卦), coupled with a 'container' at Dui 兌, will produce immensely wealthy individuals in the family.

5. Xun Formation

Sitting : **Xun 巽**   Facing : **Qian 乾**

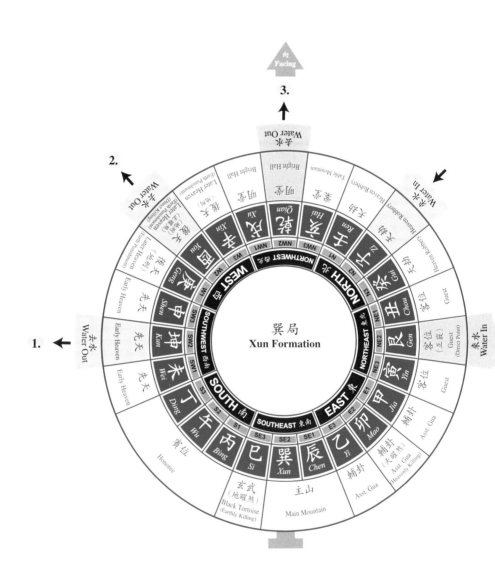

5.	Xun Formation		
Water In :	**Zi 子 , Gen 艮**	Water Out :	**Qian 乾 , You 酉 , Kun 坤**

A Dimishing Void Total Disaster Formation (消亡敗絕) will occur, in the event Incoming Kan Water, Leaving Kun (坎水流來坤位去), or Incoming Kan Water, Leaving Dui (兌), or Incoming Gen Water, Leaving Qian (乾). Furthermore, should this Water pass Through the Bright Hall (水過堂), the outcomes would be extremely inauspicious. Major chronic illness is to be expected.

6. Xun Formation

| Sitting : | **Xun 巽** | Facing : | **Qian 乾** |

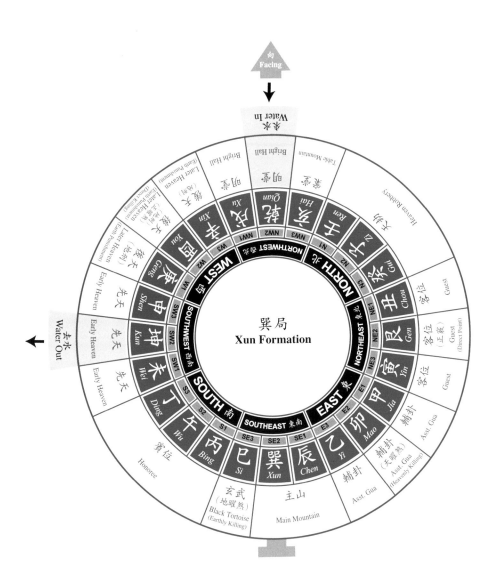

6.	Xun Formation			
	Water In :	**Qian** 乾	Water Out :	**Kun** 坤

Where Qian 乾 the Bright Hall Robbery (堂劫) and Water comes in through this direction, a case of Piercing Heart Water (穿心水) takes place. This incoming Water is an extremely inauspicious sign, as it indicates a sudden death in the family; possibly due to a landslide or being crushed by a heavy rock. (In modern times this could mean death by severe injury or earthquake or other natural disaster).

Meanwhile, Water coming in from Xu 戌 results in a case of Earthly Net (地網), which in turn, denotes imprisonment. The presence of a towering mountain or winding road at Xu 戌 indicates that one may pass away in prison, or to a less severe extent, need to be mindful of legal problems.

Water flowing directly from Xu 戌 in a most ominous sign; as it indicates that a male family member might commit suicide by hanging himself, the possibility of becoming insane, deaf or crippled, as well as being killed in a war, troubled by spiritual disturbance or suffering from a lack of intelligence.

7. Xun Formation

Sitting : **Xun 巽**　　　　Facing : **Qian 乾**

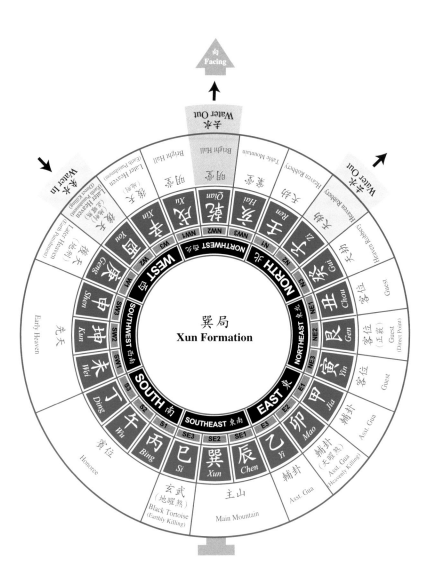

7.	Xun Formation			
Water In :	**You** 酉	Water Out :	**Qian** 乾, **Zi** 子	

Later Heaven Water from Dui Gua, Passing the Bright Hall (後天兌卦水來堂) indicates the presence of good-looking and wealthy people, although they may be lacking in intelligence. Where Water enters from Dui 兌 and exits directly from Qian 乾, one may be privileged to enjoy good beginner's luck at the initial stages of an endeavor; although such luck will eventually decline. In any case, the advent of the Dissipating Source Qi (洩盡元神) is an indicator that one's career prospects will stagnate and fail to advance.

Should Water enter from Dui 兌 and exit through Kan 坎, a case of Direct Sector (正局) Water occurs; whereby the outcomes will go against usually acceptable norms and conventions. One such example is where the family will be wealthy and prosperous, although the children in the family will tend to be rebellious and disobedient.

8. Xun Formation

Sitting : **Xun 巽**   Facing : **Qian 乾**

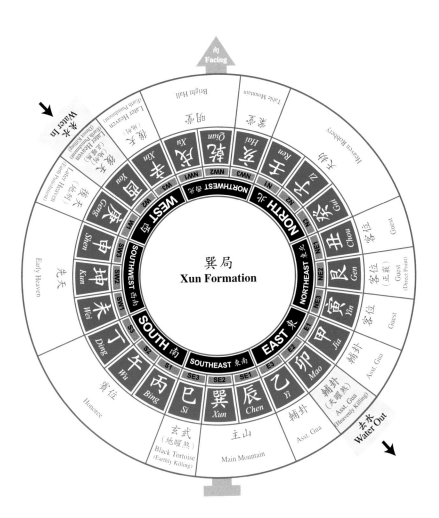

巽局
Xun Formation

8.	Xun Formation		
Water In :	**You** 酉	Water Out :	**Mao** 卯

Where Water enters from Dui 兌 and exits through Zhen 震, a scenario known as the Assistant Falls into Emptiness (輔弼落陷) takes place. This indicates the absence of assistance and helpful people in times of need, as well as poor career luck. Should Water from You, Leaving Mao (酉水來卯水去), the children in the family may be troubled by emotional problems, and also possibly suffer from insanity. Water that Exits through the Mao Direction (水出卯方) is a sign that both male and female family members may tend to behave in a lascivious or sexually immoral manner.

All of the preceding inauspicious outcomes could also occur in the event that a Punishment (刑) or Clash (沖) at Zi 子, You 酉 or Mao 卯 results in a scenario known as Filling-up Grand Duke (填實之歲君).

9. Xun Formation

Sitting : **Xun 巽** Facing : **Qian 乾**

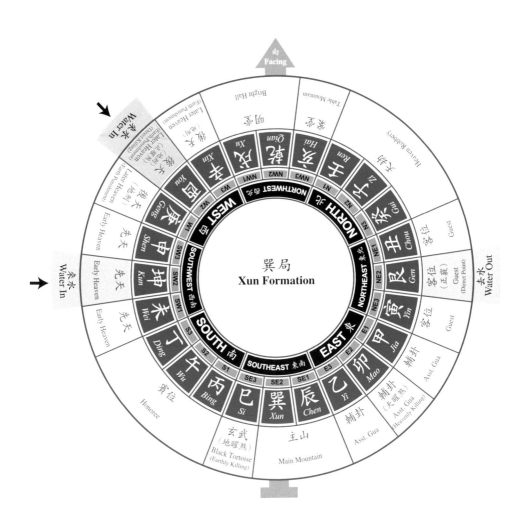

巽局
Xun Formation

9. Xun Formation

Water In : **You** 酉 **, Kun** 坤   Water Out :   **Gen** 艮

Water from Kun Gua Early Heaven, Passing through the Bright Hall (坤卦先天水朝來過堂), coupled with Water that Exits through Gen (出艮而去) is an auspicious sign, which indicates that one's family members shall prosper.

Similarly, Early Heaven Kun Water (先天坤水), combined with Later Heaven Dui Water (後天兌水) and a Gen Exit (艮) also indicates that a family will prosper accordingly. This is the primary, most important Water Mouth, as it brings about both nobility and wealth. However, one should be mindful of any sundries or a rooftop blocking this Water Mouth; as such features could bring about reverse outcomes, which include poor wealth luck and health problems.

Water Exiting through Gen (水出艮去) will also bring about prosperity for the eldest son.

10. Xun Formation

Sitting : **Xun 巽** Facing : **Qian 乾**

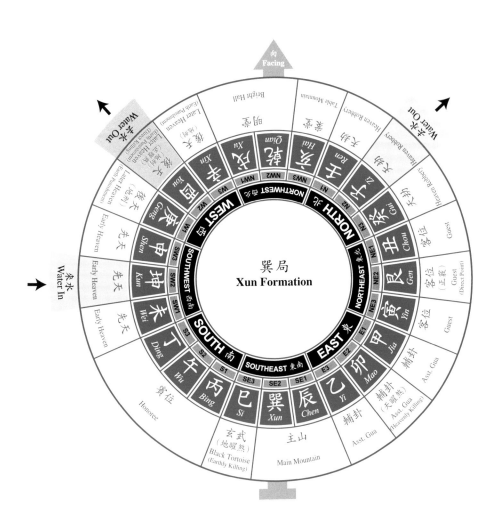

巽局
Xun Formation

10. Xun Formation

Water In : **Kun** 坤   Water Out : **You** 酉, **Zi** 子

Water from Kun Gua Early Heaven, Passing through the Bright Hall and Exiting in the Kan Direction (坤卦先天水朝來過堂) is also known as Heavenly Robbery Water (天劫水). Although this Formation will bring about auspicious outcomes, should the Water flow incorrectly or out-of-course, one's children may be inclined to behave in a rebellious or disobedient manner.

A Dui Exit (兌) will bring about extremely inauspicious outcomes, as it forms what is known as Early Heaven Clashing Out Later Heaven (先天破後天), which results in a Diminishing Void Total Disaster Formation (消亡敗絕). Furthermore, the advent of a Later Heaven Clash Out Formation (後天流破) may result in every generation of one's descendents suffering from poverty and financial difficulties. As Dui 兌 also represents younger female family members, the luck of the third son may, ironically, also decline.

11. Xun Formation

Sitting : **Xun 巽** Facing : **Qian 乾**

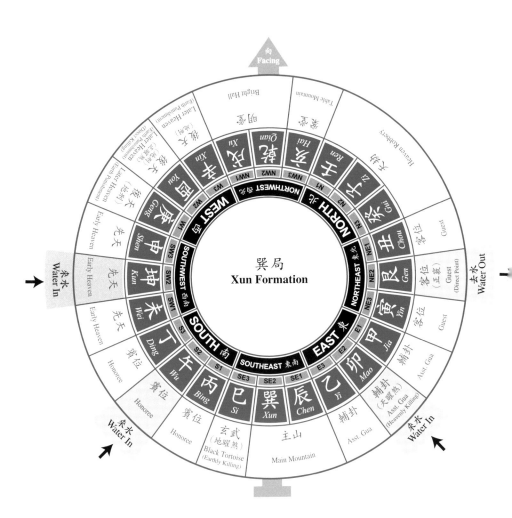

巽局
Xun Formation

11. Xun Formation

Water In : **Kun** 坤，**Wu** 午，**Mao** 卯   Water Out :   **Gen** 艮

Auspicious outcomes may be expected when Li Water (離水) flows in before turning toward Kun 坤 forms Early Heaven Water (先天水). Meanwhile, Kun Water (坤水) combines with incoming Zhen Water (震水), where Zhen 震 also represents Assistant Gua Water (輔卦水) that Passes Through Gen (歸艮而去). If all these take place, one's entire family shall prosper.

12. Xun Formation

Sitting : **Xun 巽**   Facing : **Qian 乾**

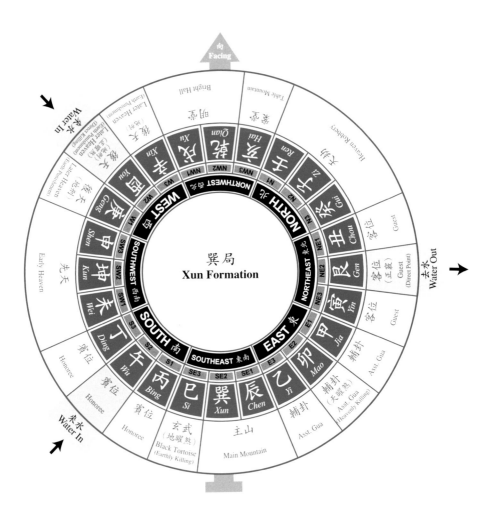

12.	Xun Formation		
Water In :	**You** 酉 , **Wu** 午	Water Out :	**Gen** 艮

Receiving Li and Dui Water, Exiting through Gen or Kan Direction (收離兌水來，歸艮 或坎方而去) is another auspicious sign, which produces wealthy, noble and intelligent family members. A Gen Exit (艮) indicates that the youngest son will be the wealthiest and most prosperous of all, while Water Exiting through Kan (出坎水) indicates that every family member shall prosper accordingly.

13. Xun Formation

Sitting : **Xun 巽**   Facing : **Qian 乾**

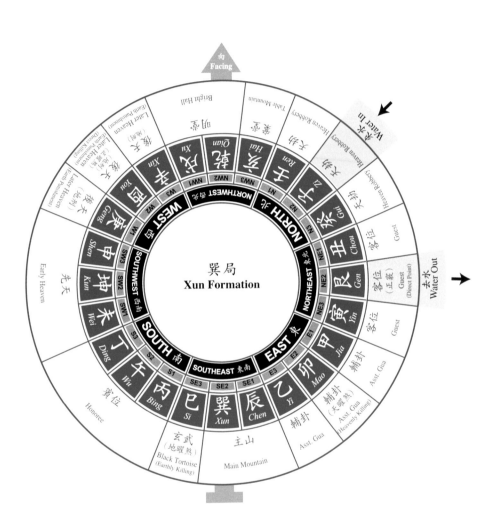

巽局
Xun Formation

13.	Xun Formation			
	Water In :	**Zi** 子	Water Out :	**Gen** 艮

Incoming Water from Kan, combining with Later Heaven Water and exiting Gen (坎水來而合先後天水歸艮而去) makes for a spot or location with excellent Feng Shui, indeed. The residents of such a place will prosper and become immensely wealthy.

The preceding scenario is also known as Dissolving Sha to Nobility (化殺爲權).

14. Xun Formation

Sitting : **Xun 巽**   Facing : **Qian 乾**

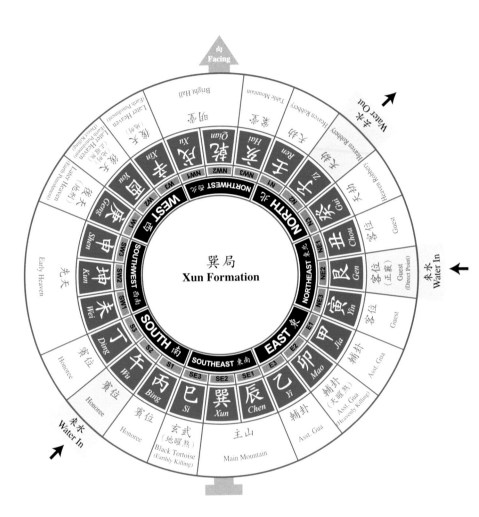

14. Xun Formation

Water In : **Wu** 午, **Gen** 艮   Water Out :   **Zi** 子

Kept Water from Li and Gen that Exits Through the Kan Direction (收離艮水來出坎方去) forms what is known as Receiving Guest Water that Exits Through Heavenly Robbery (收賓客水出天劫去). This is an inauspicious scenario, which brings about poor wealth luck and harm to one's family members. It could also lead to a family falling apart, although members of one's daughter's family will fare better than the others. The presence of adopted children, due to one's inability to sire offspring, is another possibility. This situation is also known as Internal supporting External (内益外).

15. Xun Formation

Sitting : **Xun 巽**   Facing : **Qian 乾**

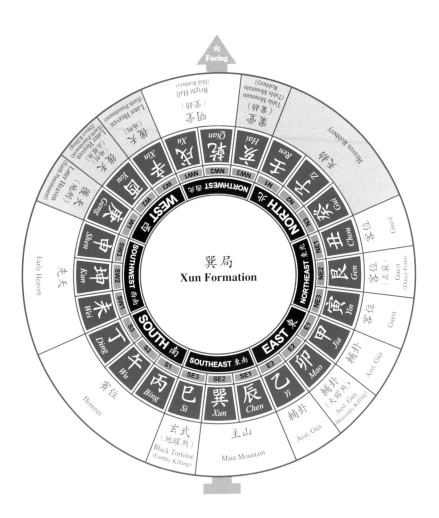

巽局
Xun Formation

15.	**Xun Formation**		
Sitting :	**Xun** 巽	Facing :	**Qian** 乾

Should one notice the presence of an oddly-shaped rock or boulder at the Heavenly Robbery Direction (天劫方), one would need to be mindful of the risk of acquiring an illness that leads to the coughing up of blood, heart diseases, as well as major accidents of any sort. There is also the possibility of encountering numerous challenges and obstacles during the latter years of one's life. Furthermore, the presence of a forest or old pine tree at the Heavenly Robbery Direction (天劫方) is the harbinger of chronic poor health and illnesses that are not easily detectable.

It would equally be possible to acquire an ailment affecting the head, chest, legs, stomach or hands, should there be a rooftop or sharp corner pointing toward the Heavenly Robbery (天劫), Earthly Punishment (地刑) or Hall Robbery 3 Positional Blade (案劫 三位刀) direction. Such health problems could also manifest themselves, where there is a pile of rocks, an old well, a handrail, a wall corner or a solid object located within a close proximity from the Bright Hall (明堂).

The presence of a Annual Grand Duke Punish-Class Sha (流年太歲刑沖殺) is the harbinger of harm befalling one's family members.

16. Xun Formation

Sitting : **Xun 巽**   Facing : **Qian 乾**

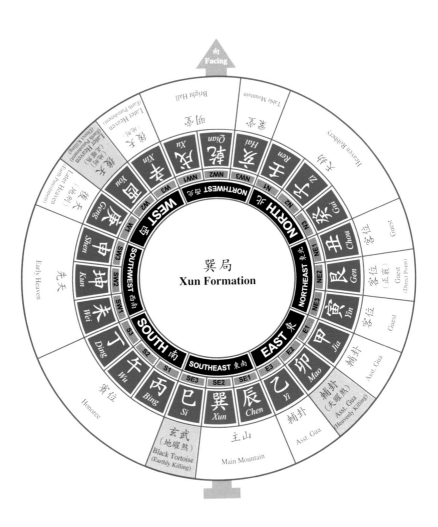

巽局
Xun Formation

16.	Xun Formation			
	Sitting :	**Xun** 巽	Facing :	**Qian** 乾

One would need to be mindful of any ailment that leads to the coughing up of blood, lung and throat disease should one notice a road, large boulder, pile of rocks, well, pylons, tree, rooftop, water-containment tower or chimney pointing toward the Shimmering Sha Direction (曜殺方). In addition, the presence of a tree at either You 酉 or Mao 卯 could bring about mental problems as well as insanity. As Mao 卯 represents the Assistant Gua Position (輔卦位) as well, this indicates poor career luck, losing one's job, and the absence of help or assistance when it is most needed.

Take note of the Grand Duke years as these will be the time where accidents and ailments occur.

However, if water is seen to enter from Kun 坤，there will be favorable outcomes at the and despite the ailments above.

7. Dui Formation 兑局

1.	**Dui Formation**			
	Sitting :	**Dui** 兌	Facing :	**Zhen** 震

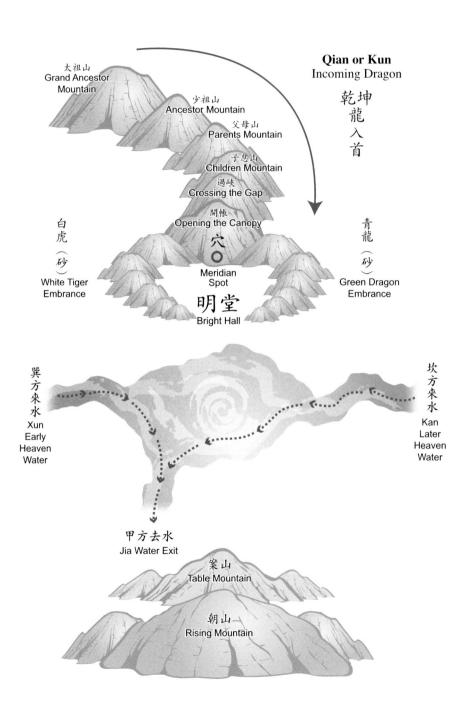

太祖山
Grand Ancestor Mountain

少祖山
Ancestor Mountain

父母山
Parents Mountain

子息山
Children Mountain

過峽
Crossing the Gap

開帳
Opening the Canopy

Qian or Kun
Incoming Dragon

乾坤龍入首

穴
○
Meridian Spot

白虎
（砂）
White Tiger Embrace

青龍
（砂）
Green Dragon Embrace

明堂
Bright Hall

巽方來水
Xun Early Heaven Water

坎方來水
Kan Later Heaven Water

甲方去水
Jia Water Exit

案山
Table Mountain

朝山
Rising Mountain

1.	**Dui Formation**		
Sitting :	**Dui 兌**	Facing :	**Zhen 震**

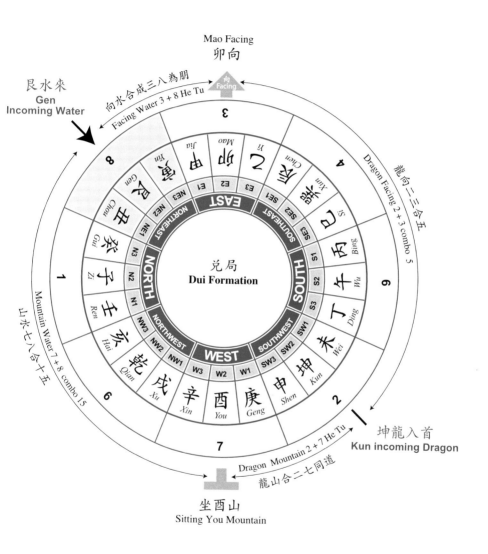

Mao Facing
卯向

艮水來
Gen Incoming Water

向水合成三八為朋
Facing Water 3 + 8 He Tu

龍向二三合五
Dragon Facing 2 + 3 combo 5

兌局
Dui Formation

山水七八合十五
Mountain Water 7 + 8 combo 15

坤龍入首
Kun incoming Dragon

Dragon Mountain 2 + 7 He Tu
龍山合二七同道

坐酉山
Sitting You Mountain

1. Dui Formation

Sitting : **Dui 兌**   Facing : **Zhen 震**

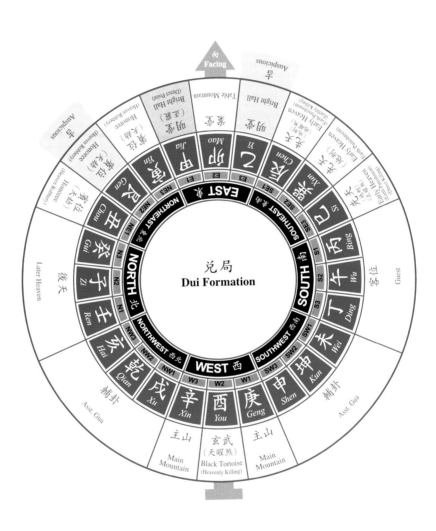

兌局
Dui Formation

1. Dui Formation

Auspicious :　　**Gen** 艮 **, Yi** 乙

If the Internal Water Structure (內局水) is located on the left, the attributes (family members) associated to the left side of the property shall prosper accordingly. Similarly, should the Internal Water Structure (內局水) happen to be located on the right, the attributes (family members) associated to the right side of the property concerned will benefit accordingly. Water that Exits directly from the Central Bright Hall (水若堂中直出) will bring about auspicious outcomes to one's son, particularly the second son.

Internal Water Exit at Jia (內程水放甲), also known as Heavenly Yuan Water (天元神水) is another auspicious scenario, as it constitutes the primary and most important Water Mouth of the Internal Sector (內局). Such a Formation brings prosperity and wealth to one's entire family. Likewise, a Exit Yi (放乙) will bring about equally auspicious outcomes, as well.

On the contrary, External Structure Water Exiting Directly from the Central Hall (外局水堂中直出) will cause one's family to fall apart and become disunited; although the second son may enjoy some measure of good luck, initially. External Structure Water flowing through the Jia Mouth (外局水流甲口) will bring about favorable outcomes to one's entire family. In fact, a Gen Exit (艮) would be most beneficial to the eldest and third sons, while a Yi Exit (乙) would be generally favorable to everyone in the family.

2. Dui Formation

| Sitting : | **Dui** 兌 | Facing : | **Zhen** 震 |

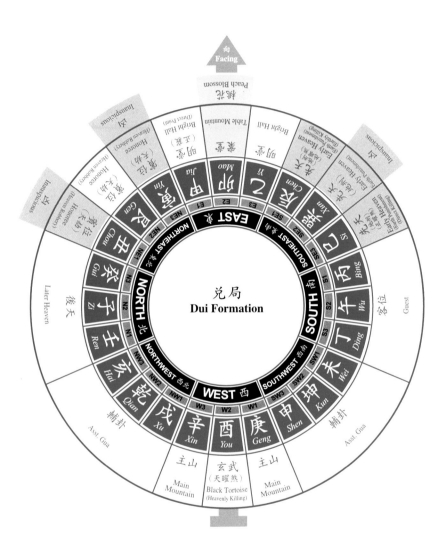

兌局
Dui Formation

2. Dui Formation

Inauspicious : **Chou** 丑, **Yin** 寅, **Xun** 巽   Peach Blossom : **Mao** 卯

One should be mindful of Internal Structure Water Released through the Xun Water Mouth (內局水放巽口), as it indicates the possibility of a miscarriage. Furthermore, female family members may suffer from hormonal imbalance and hence, health issues, where the Internal Structure flows through Branches (內程放地支).

Similarly, Water Released through Xun Gua (水放巽卦) results in what is known as Internal Structure Clashing Out Early Heaven (內局破先天). This is an undesirable scenario, as it indicates the possibility of harm befalling one's family members, more so where a Grand Duke Jupiter Clashing Punishing or Filling-in (太歲沖刑或填實) Formation is seen.

External Structure Water Flowing toward Kan (外局水流坎而去) is also known as External Structure Clashing Out Later Heaven Formation (外局破後天). This is another inauspicious scenario, which is the harbinger of a miscarriage or divorce. However, the outcomes would be most prosperous, should Water converge and be 'contained' at Kan 坎.

Water that Passes through Xun (歸巽而去) results in what is known as External Structure Clashing Out Later Heaven Formation (外局破先天). It ominously indicates the possibility of harm befalling one's family members, loss of wealth, and worse still, passing away at a relatively young age. Should such a scenario be seen, it would be advisable and prudent to cover up the Water Mouth. An Exit Li (放離) would, however, bring about auspicious outcomes.

3. Dui Formation

Sitting : **Dui 兌**   Facing : **Zhen 震**

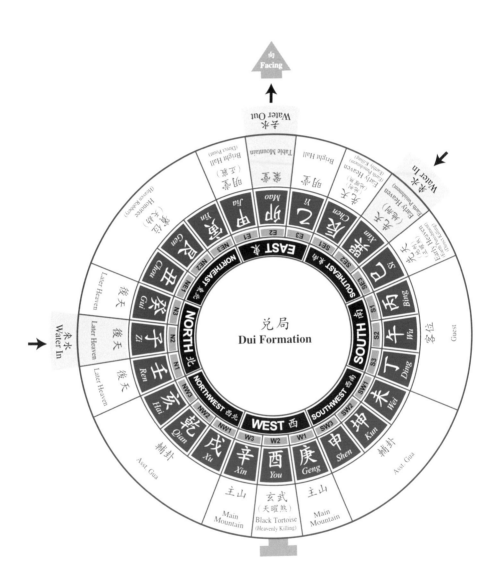

3.	Dui Formation			
	Water In :	**Zi 子,Xun 巽**	Water Out :	**Mao 卯**

Water from Early Heaven Xun, Passing through the Bright Hall (先天巽水來過堂) will bring about extremely auspicious outcomes to one's entire family. Academic achievements, in particular, will feature highly amongst the fields in which family members excel. In fact, Water from Xun Converging at Kan and Passing through Zhen (巽水來會合坎水歸) will result in one becoming wealthy, and excelling in the academic field. Such Formations indeed augur well in enhancing one's wealth prospects, as well as one's relationships with other family members.

4. Dui Formation

Sitting : **Dui 兌**   Facing : **Zhen 震**

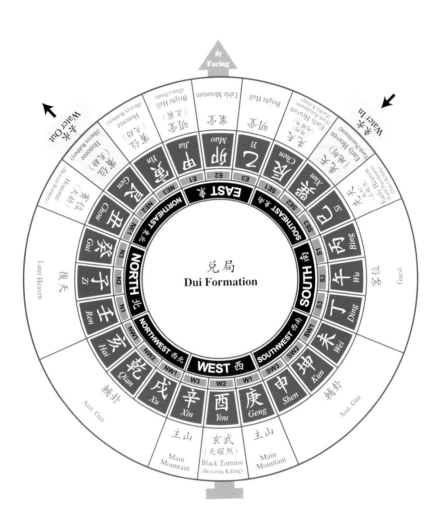

兌局
Dui Formation

4.	Dui Formation			
	Water In :	**Xun** 巽	Water Out :	**Gen** 艮

Water from Xun, Exiting through Gen (巽水來艮水) produces what is known as a Broken Structure (破局). Where such a scenario is seen, one would need to be mindful of children behaving in a rebellious manner, as well as relationship issues.

5. | Dui Formation

Sitting : **Dui 兌**   Facing : **Zhen 震**

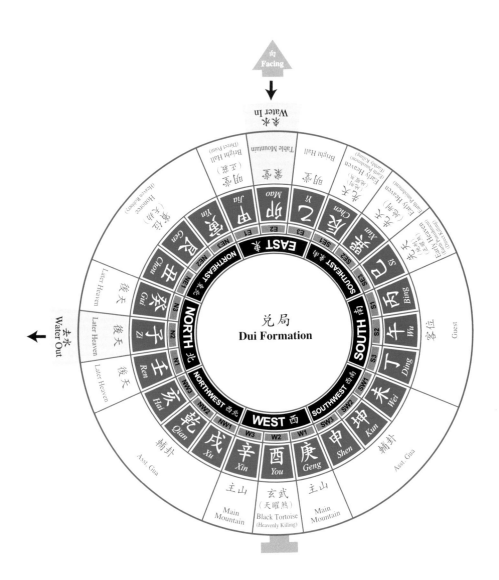

兌局
Dui Formation

240

5.	Dui Formation			
Water In :	**Mao** 卯		Water Out :	**Zi** 子

Water from the Zhen Gua Bright Hall Robbery (堂劫震卦水來) is an extremely ominous sign, as it is the harbinger of heart disease and the possibility of a sudden death in the family. In fact, Water from Zhen, Leaving Kan (震卦水來坎方去) may cause a husband to unexpectedly lose his wife, or one to behave in a sexually immoral or lascivious manner. Such a scenario could also lead to a nasty divorce.

However, should Water converge upon and be 'contained' at Kan 坎, one will prosper and become immensely wealthy; although one would still need to be mindful of meeting an untimely demise in an accident or by murder.

6. Dui Formation

Sitting : **Dui 兌** Facing : **Zhen 震**

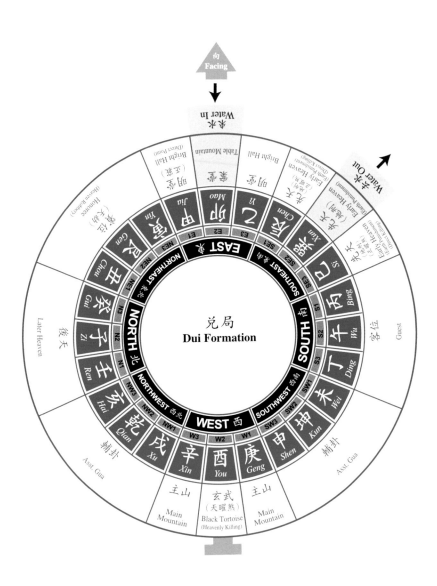

兌局
Dui Formation

6.	Dui Formation		
Water In :	**Mao** 卯	Water Out :	**Xun** 巽

Water from Zhen, Passing by and learning at Xun (震水來歸巽而去) produces what is known as an Clashing Out Early Heaven (破先天). This is an inauspicious scenario, as it indicates the possibility of one passing away at a relatively young age. In fact, the presence of an External Structure Clashing out Early Heaven (外局破先天) indicates the possibility of one being unable to sire offspring and therefore compelled to adopt children, as well as poor luck affecting one's entire family.

The presence of Peach Blossom Killing Water (桃花煞水) and Water from the Mao Period (卯水朝來) results in what is known as Salty Pool Water (咸池水). Should such a scenario be seen, female family members may tend to behave in a sexually immoral or lascivious manner, while male family members could pass away at a relatively young age. The risk of suffering from physical injury is also another possibility.

Similarly, Water from Mao Passing by Wu (卯水歸午) or Water from You Passing by Wu (酉水歸午) could result in unhealthy or immoral relationships. One such example is when female family members behave lasciviously, and elope with their lovers.

243

7. Dui Formation

Sitting : **Dui 兌**　　Facing : **Zhen 震**

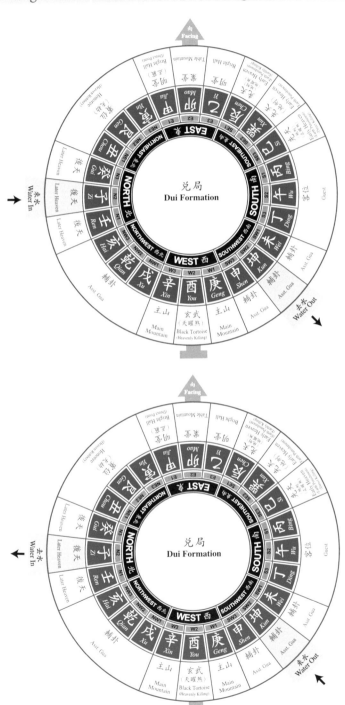

7.1	**Dui Formation**			
Water In :	**Zi** 子	Water Out :	**Kun** 坤	

7.2	**Dui Formation**			
Water In :	**Kun** 坤	Water Out :	**Zi** 子	

Incoming Water from Kan, Leaving Kun Direction (坎水來，流坤方而去) or Water from Kun, Passing Through and Flowing toward the Kan Direction (坤水來，歸坎而去) is an extremely inauspicious scenario. Where Receiving this water to the Bright Hall (收水過堂), one's fortunes and luck will eventually decline. Furthermore, should an Early and Later Heaven Clashing Out (先後天流破) be seen, one should take precautionary measures, including planting a row of trees or constructing a wall to block out this Formation.

The danger arrives an Zi 子 years where the Grand Duke resides.

8. Dui Formation

Sitting : **Dui 兑** Facing : **Zhen 震**

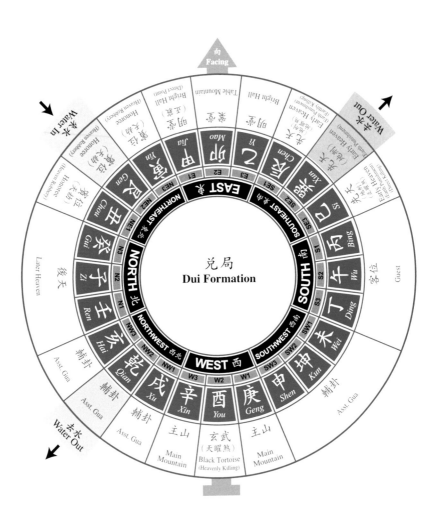

兑局
Dui Formation

8.	**Dui Formation**		
	Water In : **Gen** 艮	Water Out :	**Xun** 巽 , **Qian** 乾

Similarly, Incoming Gen Gua Water (艮卦水來) or Heavenly Robbery Water (天劫水來), Passing Through and Leaving Qian (歸乾而去) results in a Diminishing Void Total Disaster Formation. Water from Chou (丑水來) is another ominous scenario, as it is the harbinger of injuries, someone committing suicide by hanging him or herself to death, as well as fatal accidents. The presence of a hole or deep 'pit' toward the Gen Direction (艮方) is the harbinger of ailments affecting the eyes, including glaucoma and blindness. Where Incoming Yin Water (寅水來) is observed, there could also be the occurrence of a fatal accident, or death from a blood-related ailment.

Water from Gen, Passing by Xun (艮水來歸巽而去) results in what is known as 'rebellious water'. This means that one's family members could be inclined towards behaving in a rebellious or disobedient manner. Consequently, disputes would be rife, which could lead to a fall out between the siblings in a family. Furthermore, the presence of physical Sha-Qi like a high-voltage pylon or sharp rocks at either Chou 丑 or Yin 寅 is the harbinger of legal issues and problems.

9. Dui Formation

Sitting : **Dui 兌**   Facing : **Zhen 震**

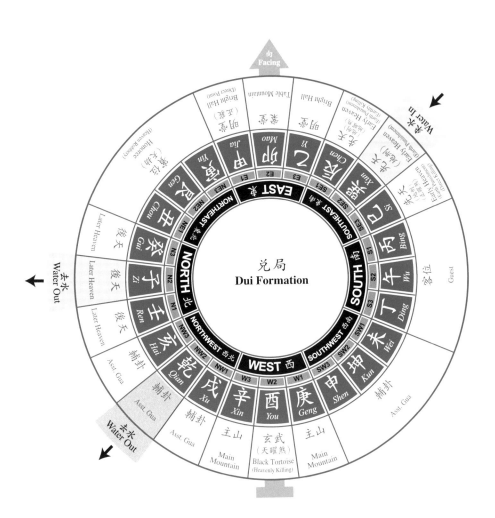

兌局
Dui Formation

9.	Dui Formation

Water In : **Xun** 巽   **Water Out :** **Zi 子, Qian** 乾

Incoming Water from Xun, Leaving Kan (巽水來坎方而去) produces what is also known as the Early Heaven Clashing Out Later Heaven (先天破後天). This is an extremely inauspicious scenario, as it is the harbinger of a miscarriage, dreadful divorce, physical injuries, as well as declining family luck.

However, where Water from Xun, Passing by the Qian Direction (巽水來歸乾方而去) is seen, prosperity and wealth shall follow suit. Unfortunately, the eldest son will not be privileged enough to enjoy correspondingly good career luck, and will therefore fail to excel or progress in his career.

10. Dui Formation

Sitting : **Dui 兑**   Facing : **Zhen 震**

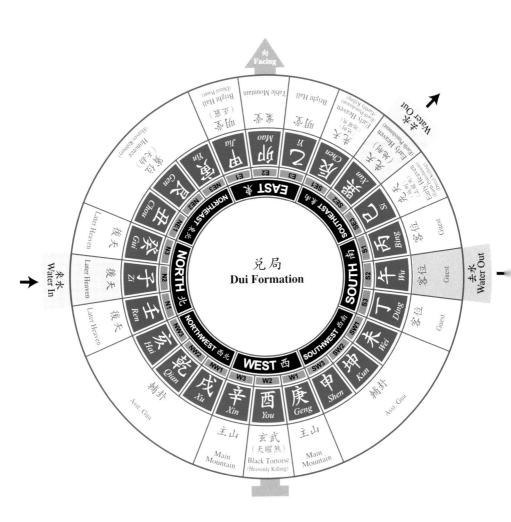

兑局
Dui Formation

10. Dui Formation

| Water In : | **Zi** 子 | Water Out : | **Xun** 巽，**Wu** 午 |

Water from Kan clashing out Xun Direction (坎水來走破巽) is another inauspicious scenario, as it indicates the possibility of a lady being widowed. Male family members may tragically pass away at a relatively young age, while the children will tend to be rebellious or disobedient to their parents. A Chen Exit (辰), would affect the second son most adversely, while a Xun Exit (巽) would be most detrimental to the eldest son. Similarly, a Si Exit (巳) would bring about unfavorable outcomes to the third son.

Water from Kan, Passing by Li (坎水來歸離而去) is also known as the Guest Position (客位). It results in a The Structure of the Borrowed Direction Point (借竅之局), which in turn, brings about extremely favorable and auspicious outcomes. Such a scenario is also identified as a Wooden City Water Shape (木城水形).

11. | Dui Formation

Sitting : **Dui** 兌   Facing : **Zhen** 震

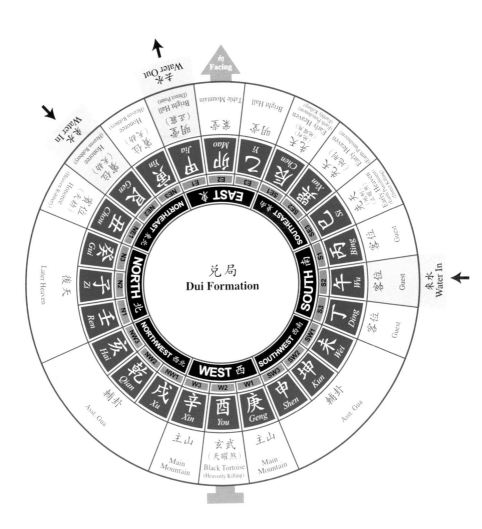

兌局
Dui Formation

11. | Dui Formation

Water In :   **Gen** 艮 , **Wu** 午   Water Out :   **Jia** 甲

Guest water clashing out Early and Later Heaven Water (收賓客水來，轉爲先後天水) that Passes through the Bright Hall (過堂) brings about auspicious outcomes. In fact, the Guest Water Assisted Structure (賓客助主), Converging with Early and Later Heaven Water (而會合先後天水) would produce the most significant, positive impact of all. This brings about great wealth, nobility and status.

12. Dui Formation

Sitting : **Dui 兌**   Facing : **Zhen 震**

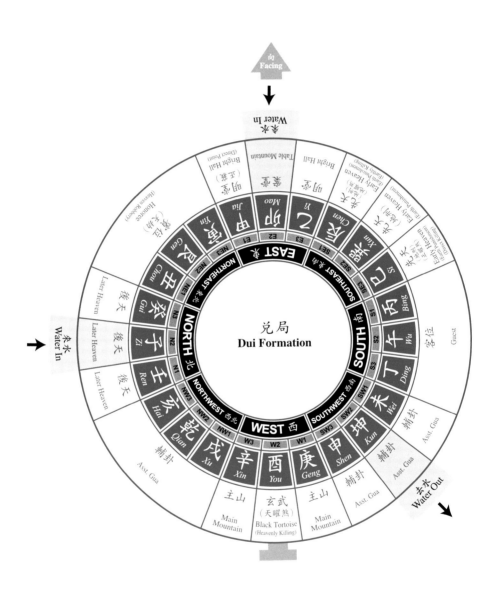

兌局
Dui Formation

12.	Dui Formation			
	Water In :	**Mao** 卯, **Zi** 子	Water Out :	**Kun** 坤

Another auspicious scenario takes place when Kan 坎 and Zhen 震 converge, resulting in a Tri-Junction Water Mouth (三叉水口) at Xun 巽, which Exits through Li, switches to exit the Kun Direction (出離而轉坤方去). Such a Formation augurs well for one's wealth and family luck. Furthermore, the presence of the 4-1 In the Same Palace (四一同宮) brings about excellent academic luck.

13. Dui Formation

Sitting :　　**Dui 兌**　　　　Facing :　　**Zhen 震**

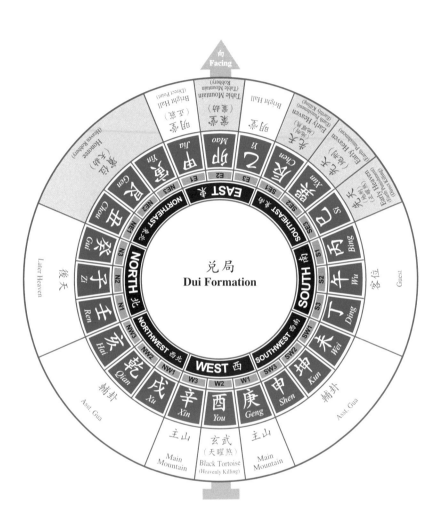

兌局
Dui Formation

13. Dui Formation

Sitting : **Dui 兌**   Facing :   **Zhen 震**

One would need to be mindful of the presence of an incoming road, such as a T-junction, or drains from either Jia 甲 or Mao 卯, Chen 辰 or Si 巳, as well as Yin 寅 or Chou 丑, as the outcomes would be extremely inauspicious. Where there is an incoming road from Jia 甲, Mao 卯 or Si 巳, one might meet with a fatal accident, or a young female family member might commit suicide by hanging herself.

Where there is an incoming road from either Yin 寅 or Jia 甲, one may be afflicted with a chronic ailment, or even become crippled or hunchbacked. An incoming road from Chou 丑 is the harbinger of chronic illnesses and injuries, while an incoming road from Chen 辰 indicates the possibility of a male family member committing suicide by hanging himself, or becoming insane.

14. Dui Formation

Sitting : **Dui 兌**   Facing : **Zhen 震**

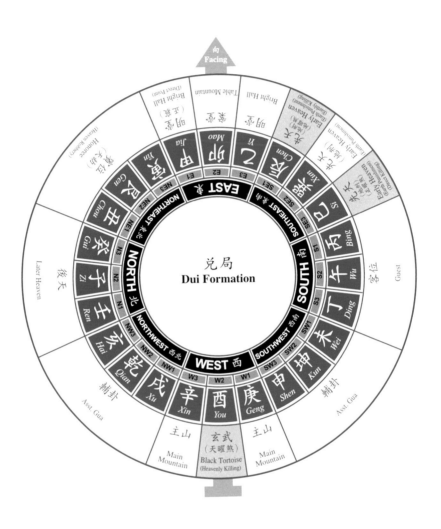

兌局
Dui Formation

14.	Dui Formation			
Sitting :	**Dui** 兌		Facing :	**Zhen** 震

Water from Chen, From the Table Mountain's Robbery Position (辰水來，堂前帶劫) is the harbinger of mental problems, as well as the possibility of being afflicted with insanity. However, if the Front of the Hall (堂前) does not coincide with the Bringing Robbery Sha (帶劫), one's luck shall be average, at best. Chen Water (辰水), coupled with a Si Robbery (巳劫), results in what is known as Si Water Chen Robbery (巳水辰劫). This is an inauspicious scenario, which brings about mental problems and insanity. Indeed, should both components have Bringing Sha (帶煞), the magnitude of such negative outcomes would be much greater.

Similarly, the presence of Sha Qi at the Shimmering Sha Robbery (劫煞曜) indicates the possibility of ailments that are not easily detectable. In fact, the presence of a large boulder, rock, or sharp or pointed corner located within close proximity from the Bright Hall (明堂) indicates that one may meet with a car accident, or suffer from an illness that leads to the coughing up of blood or the necessity of undergoing surgery. Worse still, one may tragically pass away at a relatively young age.

8. Gen Formation 艮局

1. Gen Formation

Sitting :	**Gen 艮**	Facing :	**Kun 坤**

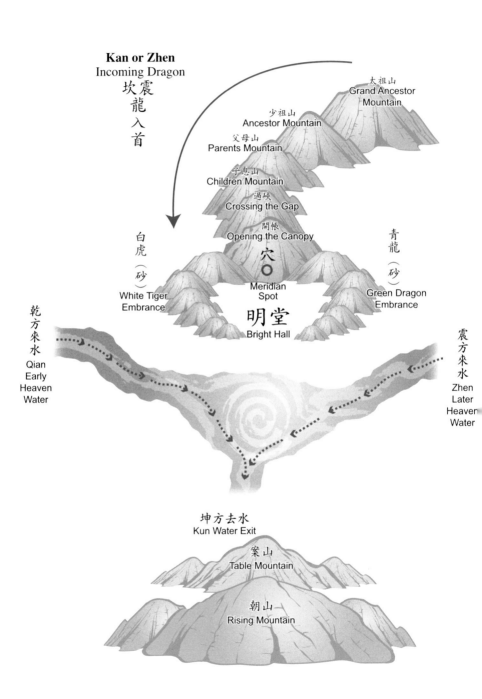

Kan or Zhen
Incoming Dragon
坎震龍入首

太祖山
Grand Ancestor Mountain

少祖山
Ancestor Mountain

父母山
Parents Mountain

子息山
Children Mountain

過峽
Crossing the Gap

開帳
Opening the Canopy

穴O
Meridian Spot

明堂
Bright Hall

白虎（砂）
White Tiger Embrance

青龍（砂）
Green Dragon Embrance

乾方來水
Qian Early Heaven Water

震方來水
Zhen Later Heaven Water

坤方去水
Kun Water Exit

案山
Table Mountain

朝山
Rising Mountain

262

1. Gen Formation

Sitting : **Gen 艮** Facing : **Kun 坤**

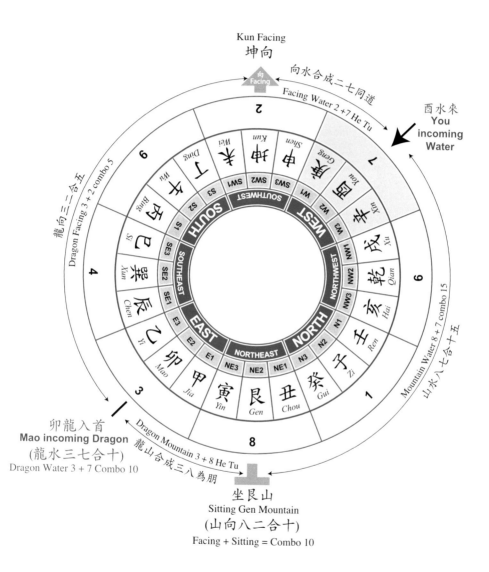

Kun Facing
坤向

向水合成二七同道
Facing Water 2 + 7 He Tu

酉水來
You incoming Water

龍向三一合五
Dragon Facing 3 + 2 combo 5

山水八七合十五
Mountain Water 8 + 7 combo 15

卯龍入首
Mao incoming Dragon
(龍水三七合十)
Dragon Water 3 + 7 Combo 10

龍山合成三八為朋
Dragon Mountain 3 + 8 He Tu

坐艮山
Sitting Gen Mountain
(山向八二合十)
Facing + Sitting = Combo 10

263

1. Gen Formation

Sitting : **Gen 艮**   Facing : **Kun 坤**

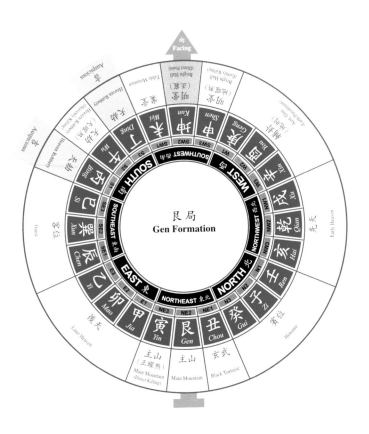

1. | Gen Formation

Auspicious : **Bing 丙, Ding 丁**

If the Internal Structure (內程) are located on the left, the attributes (family members) of the left side of the property shall prosper accordingly. Likewise, should the Internal Structure (內程) happen to be located on the right, the attributes (family members) of the right side of the property concerned will benefit accordingly. Water that Exits directly from the Central Bright Hall (水由堂中直出) will bring about auspicious outcomes to one's son, particularly the second son.

External Structure Water that changes to the Kun Position as the Exit (外局水轉坤位 出口) will also bring about prosperous outcomes to every son in the family.

Should Water Flow through the Ding Direction (水流丁位), the third and eldest sons shall enjoy good wealth and family luck. The luck of the second son's family will, however, decline. Should Water converges through Bing Direction (水歸丙方), the second son will enjoy the most favorable outcomes.

2. Gen Formation

Sitting : **Gen 艮**   Facing : **Kun 坤**

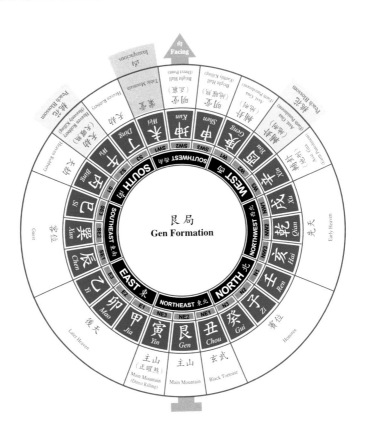

艮局
Gen Formation

2.	**Gen Formation**
	Inauspicious : **Wei** 未 Peach Blossom : **Wu** 午, **You** 酉

Water that is Exit from Wu (水放正午而出) is an auspicious scenario, which indicates that the eldest son shall prosper and become wealthy. However, as Wu 午 is also an Earthly Branch (地支), whatever wealth that is amassed may be eventually eroded. One should also be mindful of relationship issues during a Annual Year (流年), as Zi 子 shall encounter a Wu, Shen and Chen Clash. (午申辰沖).

Water that Exits through Dui Gua, Clashing with the Earthly Punishment (水出兌卦沖破地刑) is another scenario that should be avoided, as it is the harbinger of health problems affecting female family members.

The Earthly Punishment Position (地刑位) often represents Early Heaven (先天), Later Heaven (後天) or the Assistant Gua Position (輔卦位). It is important to understand that such a Formation is usually the harbinger of ailments and health problems.

3. Gen Formation

Sitting :	**Gen 艮**	Facing :	**Kun 坤**

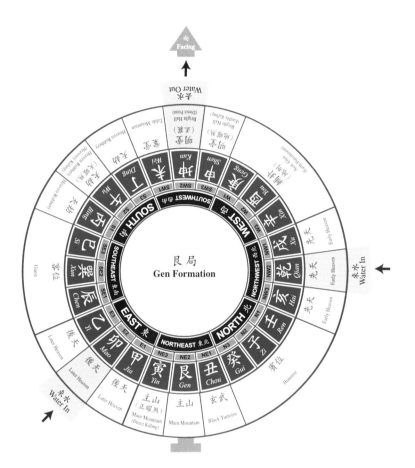

3. | Gen Formation

Water In : **Mao** 卯, **Qian** 乾   Water Out :   **Kun** 坤

The advent of Qian Water Position (乾水朝來) indicates that one's entire family shall prosper, and family members shall excel in their chosen endeavors. Qian Water Position, Converging at Later Heaven Zhen Gua Water (乾水朝來會合後天震卦水), combined with Converges at the Bright Hall and switches to Kun to exit the Direct Position (會於明堂轉坤方出中天正竅位) produces what is known as the Three Cycle Eternity Structure (三元不敗之局).

This is an auspicious Formation, which brings about wealth and prosperity to one's entire family. In fact, it is also known as the Receiving Mountain and Exiting Sha (收山出煞) method, which indicates that one's family members shall be noble, wealthy and outstanding in their pursuits. Where a Kun Position Exit Mouth (坤位出口) is seen, the presence of Embrace (砂) or a Nine Curve Exiting Water (九曲出口) will allow one's wealth to be sustained. However, should Water flow out directly, such wealth will not last for long.

4. | Gen Formation

Sitting : **Gen 艮**   Facing : **Kun 坤**

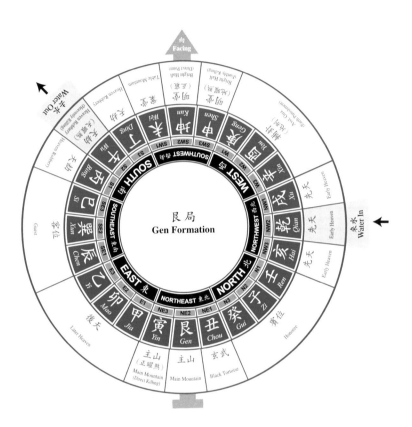

艮局
Gen Formation

4.	**Gen Formation**		
Water In :	**Qian 乾**	Water Out :	**Wu 午**

Water from Qian, Leaving Li (乾水來，離水去) results in what is known as a Diminishing Void Total Disaster Formation (消亡敗絕). Should this Water converge and Pass by the Bright Hall (過堂), one's wealth luck shall eventually decline.

Water Exit from the Ding Mouth (水放丁口) indicates that the youngest son in the family shall be noble and wealthy. Meanwhile, the eldest son's entire family will prosper, although the second son may suffer from loneliness. Water Exit from the Bing Mouth (水放丙口) would bring about the most favorable outcomes to the second son, while turning the eldest son's fortunes from poor to good. Although the eldest son's wealth luck will improve gradually, such a Formation would be least favorable in outcome to the youngest son. Water Leaving Wu Direction (水流午而去) would be most favorable to the eldest and third sons. As Wu 午 also represents Heavenly Shimmer (天曜), however, the second son may be particularly susceptible to injury during Wu 午 (Goat), and Zi 子 (Rat) years.

5. Gen Formation

Sitting : **Gen 艮**   Facing : **Kun 坤**

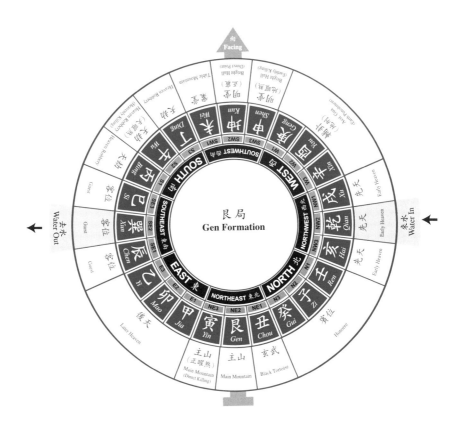

艮局
Gen Formation

5.	Gen Formation		
Water In :	**Qian 乾**	Water Out :	**Xun 巽**

Incoming Water from Qian, Leaving Xun Direction (乾水來歸巽而去) results in a Early Heaven Clashing out Guest Position Formation. Xun 巽 is also the Green Dragon Position (青龍位), which affects the eldest son the most. As this position is also identified as Borrowed Guest Water (客水借竅), it is capable of turning the eldest son's luck from good to bad. Where the Bright Hall Position (明堂位) Gathers Water As It Passes Through the Bright Hall (得水過堂), the second son's luck will turn from bad to good. Such a Formation is also known as the Borrowed from Direct Position (借竅之位). Should Chen 辰 or Si 巳 act as the Water Mouths, the outcomes would tend to be inauspicious whenever the Crashing Grand Duke (遇刑沖太歲) Formation is seen.

6. Gen Formation

Sitting : **Gen 艮** Facing : **Kun 坤**

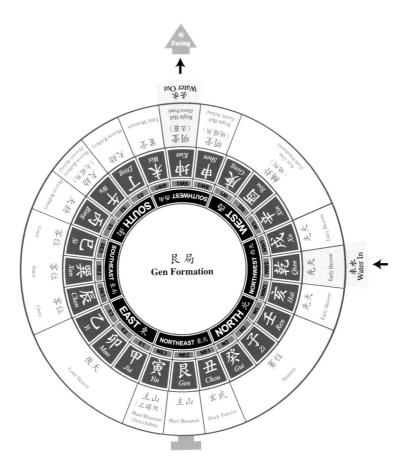

艮 局
Gen Formation

6.	Gen Formation		
Water In :	**Qian 乾**	Water Out :	**Kun 坤**

Incoming Water from Qian, Leaving Kun Direction (乾水來歸坤而去), on the contrary, will bring about extremely favorable outcomes to each and every son in the family, especially the second son. As Shen 申 also represents Shimmering Sha (曜煞), Water Exiting through the Shen Direction (水出申方) would be most favorable to the youngest son. One should, however, take extra care during Yin (Tiger) 寅 and Si (Snake) 巳 years, as harm may befall one's family members during these years. Furthermore, the presence of Reverse-Bow Water (反弓水) is the harbinger of unhealthy relationships, poor wealth luck as well as rebellious children.

7. Gen Formation

Sitting : **Gen 艮**　　　　Facing : **Kun 坤**

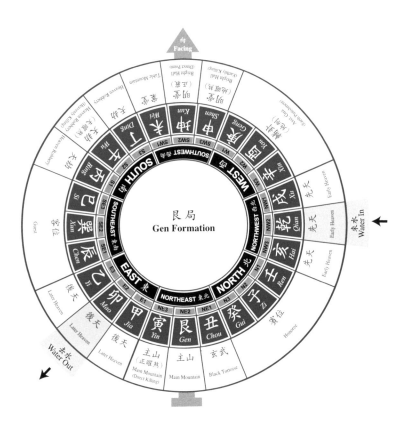

艮局
Gen Formation

7.	Gen Formation			
	Water In :	**Qian 乾**	Water Out :	**Mao 卯**

Water from Qian, Leaving Zhen (乾水來，震水去) results in what is known as External Structure Clashing Out Later Heaven (外局破後天). Should this scenario take place, one would need to be mindful of the possibility of a miscarriage, complications during pregnancy or nasty divorce. Furthermore, the luck of the eldest son may also decline. The presence of a Clash Out Later Heaven (射破後天) indicates that one may lose both his wealth and wife.

8. Gen Formation

Sitting : **Gen 艮** Facing : **Kun 坤**

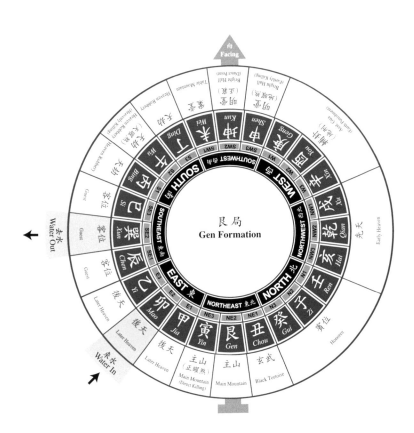

艮局
Gen Formation

8.	Gen Formation			
	Water In :	**Mao 卯**	Water Out :	**Xun 巽**

Water from Zhen to the Bright Hall (震水來上堂), coupled with Later Heaven (後天), indicates that one's wife shall be of great assistance in one's career pursuits and as such, bring one wealth and good fortune. Although the eldest son shall be privileged enough to be wealthy, he will eventually see his wealth decreasing. Where Water Passes through Xun (歸巽而去), a case of Diminishing Void Total Disaster Formation (消亡敗絕) takes place. As it affects the left side, known as the Green Dragon (青龍) of the family, the eldest son's family members shall eventually decline in numbers.

9. Gen Formation

Sitting : **Gen 艮**　　　　Facing : **Kun 坤**

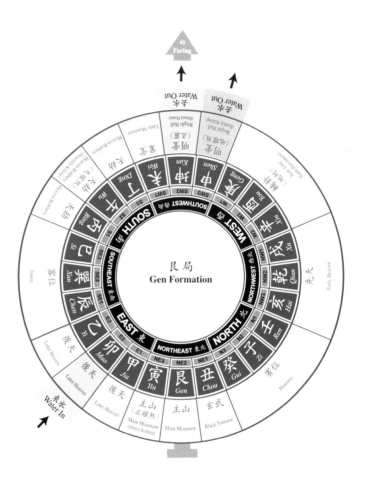

艮局
Gen Formation

9.	Gen Formation		
Water In :	**Mao** 卯	Water Out :	**Kun** 坤，**Shen** 申

Water from Zhen, Leaving Kun (震水來，坤水去) is an extremely auspicious indicator, indeed, as it is the harbinger of wealth and prosperity.

However, Water from Zhen, Exiting through the Shen Direction as the Water Mouth (震水來，出申方水口) is an inauspicious sign, as Shen 申 also represents the Shimmering Sha (曜煞) of Gen 艮.

10.	Gen Formation
Sitting :	**Gen 艮**	Facing :	**Kun 坤**

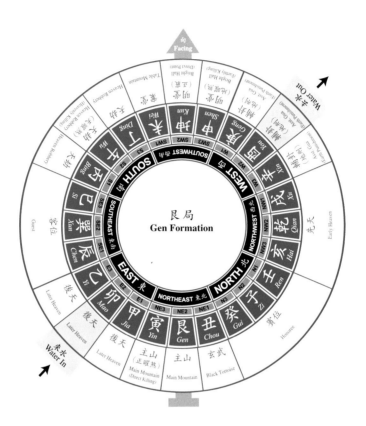

艮局
Gen Formation

10.	Gen Formation		
Water In :	**Mao** 卯	Water Out :	**You** 酉

Water from Zhen, Leaving Dui (震水來，兌水去) produces what is known as Seaming Water Passing through the Bright Hall (斜水過堂). Although Water from the Later Heaven (後天水朝來) is an indicator of wealth, such blessings may only be temporary, as the Seaming Water (水之斜) indicates a loss of wealth, or a job. In such scenarios, Dui 兌 also represents the Assistant Gua Position (輔卦位). Furthermore, in a year where a Clash and Earthly Punishment (沖破地刑) is seen, female family members may be particularly susceptible to health problems.

11. | Gen Formation

Sitting : **Gen** 艮   Facing : **Kun** 坤

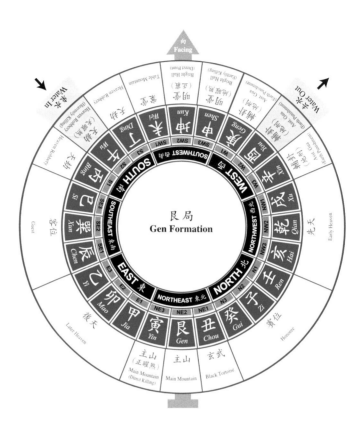

艮局
Gen Formation

11.	Gen Formation		
Water In :	**Wu** 午	Water Out :	**You** 酉

Water from Heavenly Robbery Li, Leaving Dui (天劫離水來，兌水去) produces what is known as 'Rebellious Water'. As its name implies, this indicates that one's children may tend to behave in a rebellious, disobedient manner. Meanwhile, Bing Water (丙水), also known as the Wind Sound Water (風聲水), may result in family members behaving in a flirtatious or lascivious manner. Where Water from Bing or Wu Passes by the Bright Hall (丙午水來過堂), female family members, in particular, will tend to be flirtatious or sexually immoral.

A Wu Exit (午方) or Water from a Shen Exit (申方水來), coupled with the presence of a Bright Hall Robbery (明堂帶劫), indicates the possibility of one being afflicted with insanity or mental problems.

Water from Wu (午水) indicates the possibility of imprisonment, as well as a male family members committing suicide by hanging himself.

Similarly, Heavenly Robbery Water, Passing by the Bright Hall (天劫水過堂) that coincides with a Clash-Punish Sha (沖刑殺), or a Year (歲君) of the Filling-In (填實), indicates the possibility of harm befalling one's family members.

San Yuan Dragon Gate Eight Formations Water Method 三元龍門八局水法

12. Gen Formation

| Sitting : | **Gen** 艮 | Facing : | **Kun** 坤 |

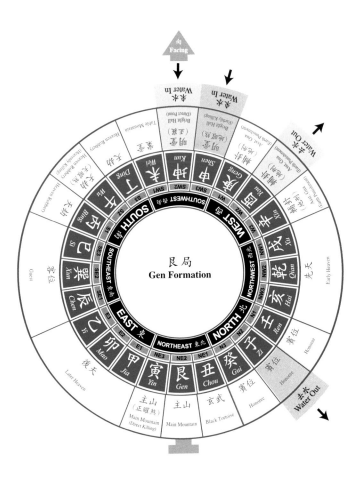

12.	Gen Formation

Water In : **Kun** 坤, **Shen** 申   Water Out : **You** 酉, **Zi** 子

As Kun 坤 also represents the Bright Hall Robbery (堂劫), Receiving Water from Kun (坤水收來) is an extremely inauspicious scenario, as it is the harbinger of heart disease, a weak heart, weak stomach, or even a sudden death in the family. Another inauspicious scenario takes place when Water from Wei, Kun or Shen, Passes through Dui (未坤申水來，歸兌而去). This results in what is known as a Diminishing Void Total Disaster Formation (消亡敗絕), whereby should Water continue to Pass through Kan (歸坎而去), the youngest son's family shall become disunited and fall apart, in due time.

Water from Wei (未水來), or an incoming road from Wei 未, could lead to one suffering from spiritual disturbances or the feeling of being 'haunted'.

Shen 申, Wu 午 and Yin 寅 also represent Shimmering Sha (曜煞). Where Water flows from Shen 申, or there is a Wu Exit Robbery (午方劫), or Incoming Wu Water (午水來), a case of what is known as a Shen Exit Robbery (申方劫) takes place. Under such circumstances, mental problems or insanity could affect one's family members.

13. Gen Formation

Sitting : **Gen 艮**   Facing : **Kun 坤**

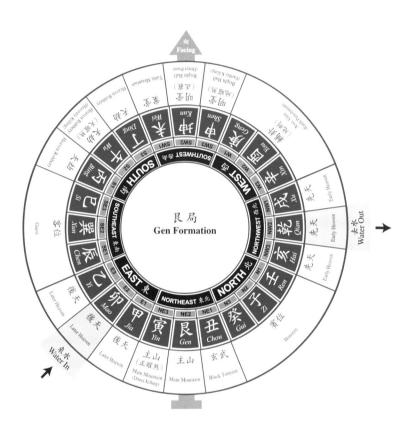

13.	Gen Formation		
Water In :	**Mao** 卯	Water Out :	**Qian** 乾

Water from Zhen, Leaving Qian (震水來，乾水去) is also known as External Structure Clashing out Early Heaven (外局破先天). This is an inauspicious sign, as it indicates that one's children may pass away at a relatively young age. However, should there be a 'container', pool or point of convergence for the Water at Qian 乾, one's entire family shall prosper. Water from Zhen (震水來) shall bring about favorable outcomes to the eldest and second sons, whereby they shall prosper accordingly. Such outcomes are, however, subject to the condition that the point of convergence or 'container' of Water must be deep and significant 'like the ocean', without any leakage which will siphon the Water outwards.

Water from Xun, Entering Kun (巽水流入坤) or Dui 兌 results in what is known as a Diminishing Void Total Disaster Formation (消亡敗絕). Likewise, Water from Li, Entering Zhen (離水流入震) or Qian 乾 will bring about a Diminishing Void Total Disaster Formation (消亡敗絕).

14. Gen Formation

Sitting : **Gen 艮**   Facing : **Kun 坤**

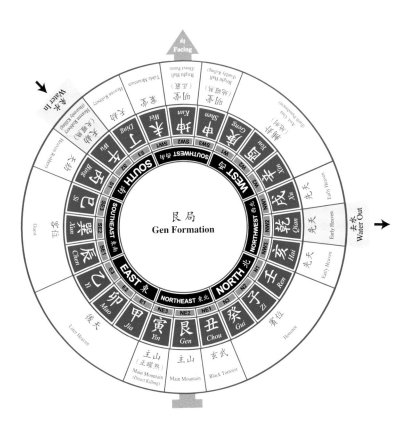

艮局
Gen Formation

14.	Gen Formation
Water In :	**Wu** 午	Water Out :	**Qian** 乾

Robbery Later Heaven Li Gua (天劫離卦水來) is the harbinger of ailments that could lead to the coughing up of blood, or Water from a Jia Exit (甲方水來), coupled with the presence of a Bright Hall Robbery (明堂帶劫), indicates the possibility of one being afflicted with insanity or mental problems.

Water from Wu (午水來) indicates the possibility of imprisonment, as well as a male family member committing suicide by hanging himself.

Similarly, Heavenly Robbery Water, Passing by the Bright Hall (天劫水過堂) that coincides with a Clash- Punish Sha (沖刑煞), or Jupiter (Year) (歲君) of the Filling-In (填實), indicates the possibility of harm befalling one's family members.

As Kun 坤 also represents the Bright Hall Robbery (堂劫), Water that Keeps Flowing from Kun (坤水收來) is an extremely inauspicious scenario, as it is the harbinger of heart disease, a weak heart, weak stomach or even a sudden death in the family. Another inauspicious scenario takes place when Water from Wei, Kun or Shen, Passes through Dui (爲坤申水來歸兌而去). This results in what is known as a Diminishing Void Total Disaster Formation (消亡敗絕), whereby should Water continue to Pass through Kan (歸坎而去), the youngest son's family shall become disunited and fall apart, in due time.

Water from Wei (未水來), or an incoming road from Wei 未, could lead to one suffering from spiritual disturbances or the feeling of being 'haunted'.

Shen 申, Wu 午 and Yin 寅 also represent Shimmering Sha (曜煞). Where Water flows from Shen 申, or there is a Wu Exit with a Robbery (午方劫), or Water flows from Wu (午水來), mental problems or insanity could affect one's family members.

15. Gen Formation

Sitting : **Gen 艮**　　Facing : **Kun 坤**

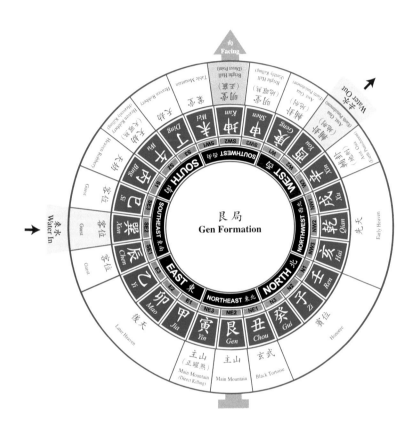

艮局
Gen Formation

15.	**Gen Formation**			
Water In :	**Xun** 巽		Water Out :	**You** 酉

One should be mindful when Xun Gua 巽卦 also represents the Guest Position (客位). Under such a circumstance, Water from Xun Gua (巽卦水來), Exit from Dui (兌方去) or Passing Through Kun (歸坤而去) would result in a Diminishing Void Total Disaster Formation (消亡敗絕). Incoming water from Xun, Leaving Xin Direction (巽水來歸 辛而去) indicates that the eldest son's family may become disunited and eventually fall apart, while unfavorable outcomes may be expected for the third son. The second son's luck, however, shall be only average.

16.	Gen Formation		
Sitting :	**Gen 艮**	Facing :	**Kun 坤**

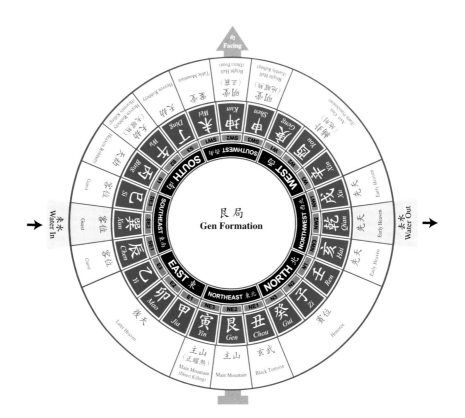

16.	Gen Formation			
Water In :	**Xun** 巽		Water Out :	**Qian** 乾

Xun Gua (巽卦) represents the Guest Position (客位), Water from Xun Gua (巽卦水來) Leaving Qian Gua (流出乾卦而去), forms a case of Favoring the Guest Over the Master (倒主陰客). Under such circumstances, the luck of one's family may decline, although one's daughter's family shall prosper. Furthermore, it indicates that one may be obliged to adopt children, to ensure the continuity of one's surname and legacy.

Water from Xun, Passing by and leaving Xu (巽水來歸戌而去) is an extremely inauspicious sign, which indicates that each and every son in the family will be prone to suffering, especially the second son. Similarly, Water Flowing Through the Qian Position (水流乾位) is the harbinger of harm befalling male family members, right from the eldest to the third sons' families.

17. Gen Formation

| Sitting : | **Gen 艮** | Facing : | **Kun 坤** |

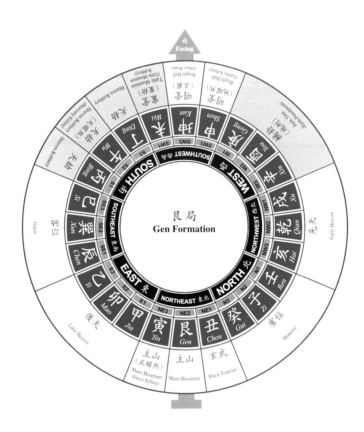

艮局
Gen Formation

17.	Gen Formation		
Sitting :	**Gen** 艮	Facing :	**Kun** 坤

Heavenly Robbery (天劫), Earthly Punishment (地刑) and Hall Robbery Sha (案劫) form what is known as a 3 Blade Table Mountain (三刀案). Where such a scenario takes place, it would be advisable to avoid having a pile of rocks, sharp boulders, T-junctions, pylons, rooftop or pointed object located within a close proximity from the Bright Hall (明堂). Failure to heed the preceding advice could lead to inauspicious outcomes, such as meeting with a car accident, having to undergo serious surgery, falling ill or getting injured. One should be all the more mindful when this circumstance coincides with a Grand Duke Jupiter Filling-up (太歲填實), or a year with a Clash- Punish Sha (沖刑 殺), as it could lead to harm befalling one's family members.

Early Later Heaven Water, Passing by the Bright Hall (先後天水過堂) that coincides with a Bright Hall (明堂) blocked by a rooftop, lamppost or dead tree is another inauspicious scenario. It is the harbinger of declining or poor luck, as well as health problems. Meanwhile, a Tight Bright Hall (明堂高壓) indicates the possibility of loneliness or being alone.

18. Gen Formation

Sitting : **Gen 艮** Facing : **Kun 坤**

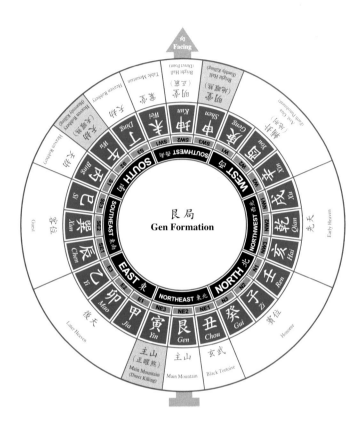

艮局
Gen Formation

18.	Gen Formation		
Sitting :	**Gen** 艮	Facing :	**Kun** 坤

The presence of a door, incoming road, tall and obstructing object, pile of sharp rocks, well, pylon, tree, pointed rooftop or large boulder at the Shimmering Sha (曜煞) indicates the onslaught of chronic ailments that could lead to the coughing up of blood.

Similarly, should there be a Shimmering Violates Killing Qi (曜位犯煞) or Robbery Water shooting through (劫水射入) the 3 Blade Table Mountain (三刀案), one may be afflicted with mental problems or even insanity, possibly due to overindulging in alcohol. Such outcomes would be even more serious and inauspicious, where all three Shimmer (曜) meet. The first Yao 曜 is the harbinger of physical sickness, the second Yao 曜 could bring about spiritual disturbance, while the third Yao 曜 is the harbinger of mental illness.

About Joey Yap

Joey Yap is the founder of the Mastery Academy of Chinese Metaphysics, a global organization devoted to the teaching of Feng Shui, BaZi, Mian Xiang and other Chinese Metaphysics subjects. He is also the Chief Consultant of Yap Global Consulting, an international consulting firm specialising in Feng Shui and Chinese Astrology services and audits.

Joey Yap is the bestselling author of over 30 books on Feng Shui, Chinese Astrology, Face Reading and Yi Jing, many of which have topped the Malaysian and Singaporean MPH bookstores' bestseller lists.

Thousands of students from all around the world have learnt and mastered Classical Feng Shui, Chinese Astrology, and other Chinese Metaphysics subjects through Joey Yap's structured learning programs, books and online training. Joey Yap's courses are currently taught by over 30 instructors worldwide.

Every year Joey Yap conducts his 'Feng Shui and Astrology' seminar to a crowd of more than 3500 people at the Kuala Lumpur Convention Center. He also takes this annual seminar on a world tour to Frankfurt, San Francisco, New York, Toronto, London, Sydney and Singapore.

In addition to being a regular guest on various radio and TV shows, Joey Yap has also written columns for The New Straits Times and The Star - Malaysia's two leading newspapers. He has also been featured in many popular global publications and networks like Time International, Forbes International, the International Herald Tribune and Bloomberg.

He has also hosted his own TV series, 'Discover Feng Shui with Joey Yap', on 8TV, a local Malaysian network in 2005; and 'Walking The Dragons with Joey Yap' on Astro Wah Lai Toi, Malaysia's cable network in 2008.

Joey Yap has worked with HSBC, Bloomberg, Microsoft, Samsung, IBM, HP, Alliance, Great Eastern, Citibank, Standard Chartered, OCBC, SIME UEP, Mah Sing, Auto Bavaria, Volvo, AXA, Singtel, ABN Amro, CIMB, Hong-Leong, Manulife and others.

Author's personal website :www.joeyyap.com

Joey Yap on Facebook:

 www.facebook.com/JoeyYapFB

EDUCATION
The Mastery Academy of Chinese Metaphysics:
the first choice for practitioners and aspiring students of the art and science of Chinese Classical Feng Shui and Astrology.

For thousands of years, Eastern knowledge has been passed from one generation to another through the system of discipleship. A venerated master would accept suitable individuals at a young age as his disciples, and informally through the years, pass on his knowledge and skills to them. His disciples in turn, would take on their own disciples, as a means to perpetuate knowledge or skills.

This system served the purpose of restricting the transfer of knowledge to only worthy honourable individuals and ensuring that outsiders or Westerners would not have access to thousands of years of Eastern knowledge, learning and research.

However, the disciple system has also resulted in Chinese Metaphysics and Classical Studies lacking systematic teaching methods. Knowledge garnered over the years has not been accumulated in a concise, systematic manner, but scattered amongst practitioners, each practicing his/her knowledge, art and science, in isolation.

The disciple system, out of place in today's modern world, endangers the advancement of these classical fields that continue to have great relevance and application today.

At the Mastery Academy of Chinese Metaphysics, our Mission is to bring Eastern Classical knowledge in the fields of metaphysics, Feng Shui and Astrology sciences and the arts to the world. These Classical teachings and knowledge, previously shrouded in secrecy and passed on only through the discipleship system, are adapted into structured learning, which can easily be understood, learnt and mastered. Through modern learning methods, these renowned ancient arts, sciences and practices can be perpetuated while facilitating more extensive application and understanding of these classical subjects.

The Mastery Academy espouses an educational philosophy that draws from the best of the East and West. It is the world's premier educational institution for the study of Chinese Metaphysics Studies offering a wide range and variety of courses, ensuring that students have the opportunity to pursue their preferred field of study and enabling existing practitioners and professionals to gain cross-disciplinary knowledge that complements their current field of practice.

Courses at the Mastery Academy have been carefully designed to ensure a comprehensive yet compact syllabus. The modular nature of the courses enables students to immediately begin to put their knowledge into practice while pursuing continued study of their field and complementary fields. Students thus have the benefit of developing and gaining practical experience in tandem with the expansion and advancement of their theoretical knowledge.

Students can also choose from a variety of study options, from a distance learning program, the Homestudy Series, that enables study at one's own pace or intensive foundation courses and compact lecture-based courses, held in various cities around the world by Joey Yap or our licensed instructors. The Mastery Academy's faculty and make-up is international in nature, thus ensuring that prospective students can attend courses at destinations nearest to their country of origin or with a licensed Mastery Academy instructor in their home country.

The Mastery Academy provides 24x7 support to students through its Online Community, with a variety of tools, documents, forums and e-learning materials to help students stay at the forefront of research in their fields and gain invaluable assistance from peers and mentoring from their instructors.

TM

MASTERY ACADEMY
OF CHINESE METAPHYSICS

www.masteryacademy.com

MALAYSIA
19-3, The Boulevard
Mid Valley City
59200 Kuala Lumpur, Malaysia
Tel : +603-2284 8080
Fax : +603-2284 1218
Email : info@masteryacademy.com

Australia, Austria, Canada, China, Croatia, Cyprus, Czech Republic, Denmark, France, Germany, Greece, Hungary, India, Italy, Kazakhstan, Malaysia, Netherlands (Holland), New Zealand, Philippines, Poland, Russian Federation, Singapore, Slovenia, South Africa, Switzerland, Turkey, U.S.A., Ukraine, United Kingdom

Introducing...
The Mastery Academy's E-Learning Center!

The Mastery Academy's goal has always been to share authentic knowledge of Chinese Metaphysics with the whole world.

Nevertheless, we do recognize that distance, time, and hotel and traveling costs – amongst many other factors – could actually hinder people from enrolling for a classroom-based course. But with the advent and amazing advance of IT today, NOT any more!

With this in mind, we have invested heavily in IT, to conceive what is probably the first and only E-Learning Center in the world today that offers a full range of studies in the field of Chinese Metaphysics.

Convenient   Study from Your Own Home   Easy Enrollment

The Mastery Academy's E-Learning Center

Now, armed with your trusty computer or laptop, and Internet access, knowledge of classical Feng Shui, BaZi (Destiny Analysis) and Mian Xiang (Face Reading) are but a literal click away!

Study at your own pace, and interact with your Instructor and fellow students worldwide, from anywhere in the world. With our E-Learning Center, knowledge of Chinese Metaphysics is brought DIRECTLY to you in all its clarity – topic-by-topic, and lesson-by-lesson; with illustrated presentations and comprehensive notes expediting your learning curve!

Your education journey through our E-Learning Center may be done via any of the following approaches:

1. Online Courses

There are 3 Programs available: our Online Feng Shui Program, Online BaZi Program, and Online Mian Xiang Program. Each Program consists of several Levels, with each Level consisting of many Lessons in turn. Each Lesson contains a pre-recorded video session on the topic at hand, accompanied by presentation-slides and graphics as well as downloadable tutorial notes that you can print and file for future reference.

Video Lecture

Presentation Slide

Downloadable Notes

2. MA Live!

MA Live!, as its name implies, enables LIVE broadcasts of Joey Yap's courses and seminars – right to your computer screen. Students will not only get to see and hear Joey talk on real-time `live`, but also participate and more importantly, TALK to Joey via the MA Live! interface. All the benefits of a live class, minus the hassle of actually having to attend one!

How It Works   1.

2.

Our Live Classes   You at Home

3. Video-On-Demand (VOD)

Get immediate streaming-downloads of the Mastery Academy's wide range of educational DVDs, right on your computer screen. No more shipping costs and waiting time to be incurred!

Instant VOD Online   1.

2.

Choose From Our list of Available VODs!   Click "Play" on Your PC

Welcome to **www.maelearning.com**; the web portal of our E-Learning Center, and YOUR virtual gateway to Chinese Metaphysics!

Mastery Academy around the world

Canada

United States

Denmark
Czech Republic
Austria
Switzerland
Poland
United Kingdom
Netherlands
Germany
Solvenia
France
Italy
Hungary
Croatia
Cyprus
Greece

Russian
Federation
Ukraine
Turkey
Kazakhstan
India

China

Philippines
Kuala Lumpur
Malaysia
Singapore

South Africa

Australia

New Zealand

YAP GLOBAL CONSULTING

Joey Yap & Yap Global Consulting

Headed by Joey Yap, Yap Global Consulting (YGC) is a leading international consulting firm specializing in Feng Shui, Mian Xiang (Face Reading) and BaZi (Destiny Analysis) consulting services worldwide. Joey Yap - an internationally renowned Master Trainer, Consultant, Speaker and best-selling Author - has dedicated his life to the art and science of Chinese Metaphysics.

YGC has its main office in Kuala Lumpur, and draws upon its diverse reservoir of strength from a group of dedicated and experienced consultants based in more than 30 countries, worldwide.

As the pioneer in blending established, classical Chinese Metaphysics techniques with the latest approach in consultation practices, YGC has built its reputation on the principles of professionalism and only the highest standards of service. This allows us to retain the cutting edge in delivering Feng Shui and Destiny consultation services to both corporate and personal clients, in a simple and direct manner, without compromising on quality.

Across Industries: Our Portfolio of Clients

Our diverse portfolio of both corporate and individual clients from all around the world bears testimony to our experience and capabilities.

Virtually every industry imaginable has benefited from our services - ranging from academic and financial institutions, real-estate developers and multinational corporations, to those in the leisure and tourism industry. Our services are also engaged by professionals, prominent business personalities, celebrities, high-profile politicians and people from all walks of life.

YAP GLOBAL CONSULTING

e (Mr./Mrs./Ms.):_____

act Details

_____ Fax:_____

le :_____

il:_____

: Type of Consultation Are You Interested In?

ng Shui ☐ BaZi ☐ Date Selection ☐ Yi Jing

e tick if applicable:

re you a Property Developer looking to engage Yap Global
onsulting?

re you a Property Investor looking for tailor-made pack-
es to suit your investment requirements?

Please attach your name card here.

Thank you for completing this form. Please fax it back to us at:

Malaysia & the rest of the world
Fax : +603-2284 2213   Tel : +603-2284 1213

www.joeyyap.com

Feng Shui Consultations

For Residential Properties
- Initial Land/Property Assessment
- Residential Feng Shui Consultations
- Residential Land Selection
- End-to-End Residential Consultation

For Commercial Properties
- Initial Land/Property Assessment
- Commercial Feng Shui Consultations
- Commercial Land Selection
- End-to-End Commercial Consultation

For Property Developers
- End-to-End Consultation
- Post-Consultation Advisory Services
- Panel Feng Shui Consultant

For Property Investors
- Your Personal Feng Shui Consultant
- Tailor-Made Packages

For Memorial Parks & Burial Sites
- Yin House Feng Shui

BaZi Consultations

Personal Destiny Analysis
- Personal Destiny Analysis for Individuals
- Children's BaZi Analysis
- Family BaZi Analysis

Strategic Analysis for Corporate Organizations
- Corporate BaZi Consultations
- BaZi Analysis for Human Resource Management

Entrepreneurs & Business Owners
- BaZi Analysis for Entrepreneurs

Career Pursuits
- BaZi Career Analysis

Relationships
- Marriage and Compatibility Analysis
- Partnership Analysis

For Everyone
- Annual BaZi Forecast
- Your Personal BaZi Coach

Date Selection Consultations

- **Marriage Date Selection**
- **Caesarean Birth Date Selection**
- **House-Moving Date Selection**
- **Renovation & Groundbreaking Dates**

- **Signing of Contracts**
- **Official Openings**
- **Product Launches**

Yi Jing Assessment

A Time-Tested, Accurate Science

- With a history predating 4 millennia, the Yi Jing - or Classic of Change - is one of the oldest Chinese texts surviving today. Its purpose as an oracle, in predicting the outcome of things, is based on the variables of Time, Space and Specific Events.

- A Yi Jing Assessment provides specific answers to any specific questions you may have about a specific event or endeavor. This is something that a Destiny Analysis would not be able to give you.

Basically, what a Yi Jing Assessment does is focus on only ONE aspect or item at a particular point in your life, and give you a calculated prediction of the details that will follow suit, if you undertake a particular action. It gives you an insight into a situation, and what course of action to take in order to arrive at a satisfactory outcome at the end of the day.

Please Contact YGC for a personalized Yi Jing Assessment!

INVITING US TO YOUR CORPORATE EVENTS

Many reputable organizations and institutions have worked closely with YGC to build a synergistic business relationship by engaging our team of consultants, led by Joey Yap, as speakers at their corporate events. Our seminars and short talks are always packed with audiences consisting of clients and associates of multinational and public-listed companies as well as key stakeholders of financial institutions.

We tailor our seminars and talks to suit the anticipated or pertinent group of audience. Be it a department, subsidiary, your clients or even the entire corporation, we aim to fit your requirements in delivering the intended message(s).

Tel: +603-2284 1213   Email: consultation@joeyyap.com

CHINESE METAPHYSICS REFERENCE SERIES

The Chinese Metaphysics Reference Series is a collection of reference texts, source material, and educational textbooks to be used as supplementary guides by scholars, students, researchers, teachers and practitioners of Chinese Metaphysics.

These comprehensive and structured books provide fast, easy reference to aid in the study and practice of various Chinese Metaphysics subjects including Feng Shui, BaZi, Yi Jing, Zi Wei, Liu Ren, Ze Ri, Ta Yi, Qi Men and Mian Xiang.

The Chinese Metaphysics Compendium

At over 1,000 pages, the *Chinese Metaphysics Compendium* is a unique one-volume reference book that compiles all the formulas relating to Feng Shui, BaZi (Four Pillars of Destiny), Zi Wei (Purple Star Astrology), Yi Jing (I-Ching), Qi Men (Mystical Doorways), Ze Ri (Date Selection), Mian Xiang (Face Reading) and other sources of Chinese Metaphysics.

It is presented in the form of easy-to-read tables, diagrams and reference charts, all of which are compiled into one handy book. This first-of-its-kind compendium is presented in both English and the original Chinese, so that none of the meanings and contexts of the technical terminologies are lost.

The only essential and comprehensive reference on Chinese Metaphysics, and an absolute must-have for all students, scholars, and practitioners of Chinese Metaphysics.

The Ten Thousand Year Calendar

Dong Gong Date Selection

The Date Selection Compendium

Plum Blossoms Divination Reference Book

San Yuan Dragon Gate Eight Formations Water Method

Xuan Kong Da Gua Ten Thousand Year Calendar

Xuan Kong Da Gua Structures Reference Book

Xuan Kong Da Gua 64 Gua Transformation Analysis

Xuan Kong Purple White Script

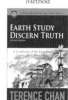
Earth Study Discern Truth Second Edition

Bazi Structures and Structural Useful Gods - Wood

Bazi Structures and Structural Useful Gods - Fire

Bazi Structures and Structural Useful Gods - Earth

Bazi Structures and Structural Useful Gods - Metal

Bazi Structures and Structural Useful Gods - Water

Educational Tools & Software

Xuan Kong Flying Stars Feng Shui Software
The Essential Application for Enthusiasts and Professionals

The Xuan Kong Flying Stars Feng Shui Software is a brand-new application by Joey Yap that will assist you in the practice of Xuan Kong Feng Shui with minimum fuss and maximum effectiveness. Superimpose the Flying Stars charts over your house plans (or those of your clients) to clearly demarcate the 9 Palaces. Use it to help you create fast and sophisticated chart drawings and presentations, as well as to assist professional practitioners in the report-writing process before presenting the final reports for your clients. Students can use it to practice their Xuan Kong Feng Shui skills and knowledge, and it can even be used by designers and architects!

Some of the highlights of the software include:
- Natal Flying Stars
- Monthly Flying Stars
- 81 Flying Stars Combinations
- Dual-View Format
- Annual Flying Stars
- Flying Stars Integration
- 24 Mountains

All charts will be are printable and configurable, and can be saved for future editing. Also, you'll be able to export your charts into most image file formats like jpeg, bmp, and gif.

The Xuan Kong Flying Stars Feng Shui Software can make your Feng Shui practice simpler and more effective, garnering you amazing results with less effort!

Mini Feng Shui Compass

This Mini Feng Shui Compass with the accompanying Companion Booklet written by leading Feng Shui and Chinese Astrology Master Trainer Joey Yap is a must-have for any Feng Shui enthusiast.

The Mini Feng Shui Compass is a self-aligning compass that is not only light at 100gms but also built sturdily to ensure it will be convenient to use anywhere. The rings on the Mini Feng Shui Compass are bilingual and incorporate the 24 Mountain Rings that is used in your traditional Luo Pan.

The comprehensive booklet included will guide you in applying the 24 Mountain Directions on your Mini Feng Shui Compass effectively and the 8 Mansions Feng Shui to locate the most auspicious locations within your home, office and surroundings. You can also use the Mini Feng Shui Compass when measuring the direction of your property for the purpose of applying Flying Stars Feng Shui.

Educational Tools & Software

BaZi Ming Pan Software Version 2.0
Professional Four Pillars Calculator for Destiny Analysis

The BaZi Ming Pan Version 2.0 Professional Four Pillars Calculator for Destiny Analysis is the most technically advanced software of its kind in the world today. It allows even those without any knowledge of BaZi to generate their own BaZi Charts, and provides virtually every detail required to undertake a comprehensive Destiny Analysis.

This Professional Four Pillars Calculator allows you to even undertake a day-to-day analysis of your Destiny. What's more, all BaZi Charts generated by this software are fully printable and configurable! Designed for both enthusiasts and professional practitioners, this state-of-the-art software blends details with simplicity, and is capable of generating 4 different types of BaZi charts: **BaZi Professional Charts, BaZi Annual Analysis Charts, BaZi Pillar Analysis Charts and BaZi Family Relationship Charts.**

Additional references, configurable to cater to all levels of BaZi knowledge and usage, include:
• Dual Age & Bilingual Option (Western & Chinese) • Na Yin narrations • 12 Life Stages evaluation • Death & Emptiness • Gods & Killings • Special Days • Heavenly Virtue Nobles

This software also comes with a Client Management feature that allows you to save and trace clients' records instantly, navigate effortlessly between BaZi charts, and file your clients' information in an organized manner.

The BaZi Ming Pan Version 2.0 Calculator sets a new standard by combining the best of BaZi and technology.

Joey Yap Feng Shui Template Set

Directions are the cornerstone of any successful Feng Shui audit or application. The **Joey Yap Feng Shui Template Set** is a set of three templates to simplify the process of taking directions and determining locations and positions, whether it's for a building, a house, or an open area such as a plot of land, all with just a floor plan or area map.

The Set comprises 3 basic templates: The Basic Feng Shui Template, 8 Mansions Feng Shui Template, and the Flying Stars Feng Shui Template.

With bi-lingual notations for these directions; both in English and the original Chinese, the **Joey Yap Feng Shui Template Set** comes with its own Booklet that gives simple yet detailed instructions on how to make use of the 3 templates within.

• Easy-to-use, simple, and straightforward
• Small and portable; each template measuring only 5" x 5"
• Additional 8 Mansions and Flying Stars Reference Rings
• Handy companion booklet with usage tips and examples

Accelerate Your Face Reading Skills With
Joey Yap's Face Reading Revealed DVD Series

Mian Xiang, the Chinese art of Face Reading, is an ancient form of physiognomy and entails the use of the face and facial characteristics to evaluate key aspects of a person's life, luck and destiny. In his Face Reading DVDs series, Joey Yap shows you how the facial features reveal a wealth of information about a person's luck, destiny and personality.

Mian Xiang also tell us the talents, quirks and personality of an individual. Do you know that just by looking at a person's face, you can ascertain his or her health, wealth, relationships and career? Let Joey Yap show you how the 12 Palaces can be utilised to reveal a person's inner talents, characteristics and much more.

Each facial feature on the face represents one year in a person's life. Your face is a 100-year map of your life and each position reveals your fortune and destiny at a particular age as well as insights and information about your personality, skills, abilities and destiny.

Using Mian Xiang, you will also be able to plan your life ahead by identifying, for example, the right business partner and knowing the sort of person that you need to avoid. By knowing their characteristics through the facial features, you will be able to gauge their intentions and gain an upper hand in negotiations.

Do you know what moles signify? Do they bring good or bad luck? Do you want to build better relationships with your partner or family members or have your ever wondered why you seem to be always bogged down by trivial problems in your life?

In these highly entertaining DVDs, Joey will help you answer all these questions and more. You will be able to ascertain the underlying meaning of moles, birthmarks or even the type of your hair in Face Reading. Joey will also reveal the guidelines to help you foster better and stronger relationships with your loved ones through Mian Xiang.

Feng Shui for Homebuyers DVD Series

Best-selling Author, and international Master Trainer and Consultant Joey Yap reveals in these DVDs the significant Feng Shui features that every homebuyer should know when evaluating a property.

Joey will guide you on how to customise your home to maximise the Feng Shui potential of your property and gain the full benefit of improving your health, wealth and love life using the 9 Palace Grid. He will show you how to go about applying the classical applications of the Life Gua and House Gua techniques to get attuned to your Sheng Qi (positive energies).

In these DVDs, you will also learn how to identify properties with good Feng Shui features that will help you promote a fulfilling life and achieve your full potential. Discover how to avoid properties with negative Feng Shui that can bring about detrimental effects to your health, wealth and relationships.

Joey will also elaborate on how to fix the various aspects of your home that may have an impact on the Feng Shui of your property and give pointers on how to tap into the positive energies to support your goals.

Discover Feng Shui with Joey Yap (TV Series)

Discover Feng Shui with Joey Yap: Set of 4 DVDs

Informative and entertaining, classical Feng Shui comes alive in *Discover Feng Shui with Joey Yap!*

Dying to know how you can use Feng Shui to improve your house or office, but simply too busy attend for formal classes?

You have the questions. Now let Joey personally answer them in this 4-set DVD compilation! Learn how to ensure the viability of your residence or workplace, Feng Shui-wise, without having to convert it into a Chinese antiques' shop. Classical Feng Shui is about harnessing the natural power of your environment to improve quality of life. It's a systematic and subtle metaphysical science.

And that's not all. Joey also debunks many a myth about classical Feng Shui, and shares with viewers Face Reading tips as well!

Own the series that national channel 8TV did a re-run of in 2005, today!

Continue Your Journey with Joey Yap's Books

Pure Feng Shui

Pure Feng Shui is Joey Yap's debut with an international publisher, CICO Books, and is a refreshing and elegant look at the intricacies of Classical Feng Shui – now compiled in a useful manner for modern-day readers. This book is a comprehensive introduction to all the important precepts and techniques of Feng Shui practice.

He reveals how to use Feng Shui to bring prosperity, good relationships, and success into one's life the simple and genuine way – without having to resort to symbols or figurines! He shows readers how to work with what they have and make simple and sustainable changes that can have significant Feng Shui effect. The principles of Classical Feng Shui and Chinese Astrology inform his teachings and explanations, so all that the readers need are a compass, a pencil, some paper, and an open mind!

Joey Yap's Art of Face Reading

The Art of Face Reading is Joey Yap's second effort with CICO Books, and takes a lighter, more practical approach to Face Reading. This book does not so much focus on the individual features as it does on reading the entire face. It is about identifying common personality types and characters.

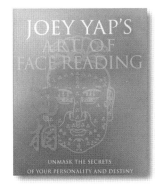

Joey shows readers how to identify successful career faces, or faces that are most likely to be able to do well financially. He also explores Face Reading in the context of health. He uses examples of real people - famous and ordinary folk - to allow readers to better understand what these facial features look like on an actual face. Readers will learn how to identify faces in Career, Wealth, Relationships, and Health (eg. 'The Salesperson Face,' 'The Politician Face,' 'The Unfaithful One,' 'The Shopaholic One,' and plenty more.)

Continue Your Journey with Joey Yap's Books

Easy Guide on Face Reading (English & Chinese versions)

The Face Reading Essentials series of books comprise 5 individual books on the key features of the face – Eyes, Eyebrows, Ears, Nose, and Mouth. Each book provides a detailed illustration and a simple yet descriptive explanation on the individual types of the features.

The books are equally useful and effective for beginners, enthusiasts, and the curious. The series is designed to enable people who are new to Face Reading to make the most of first impressions and learn to apply Face Reading skills to understand the personality and character of friends, family, co-workers, and even business associates.

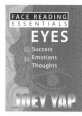 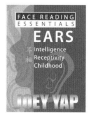 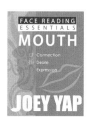 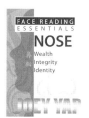 

BaZi Essentials Series (English & Chinese versions)

The BaZi Essentials series of books comprise 10 individual books that focus on the individual Day Masters in BaZi (Four Pillars of Destiny, or Chinese Astrology) study and analysis. With each book focusing on one particular Day Master, Joey explains why the Day Master is the fundamental starting point for BaZi analysis, and is the true essence of one's character traits and basic identity.

With these concise and entertaining books that are designed to be both informative and entertaining, Joey shows how each person is different and unique, yet share similar traits, according to his or her respective Day Master. These 10 guides will provide crucial insight into why people behave in the various different ways they do.

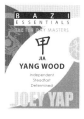    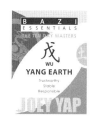

Continue Your Journey with Joey Yap's Books

Get to know your BaZi Structure... and Understand How You Approach the World

Joey Yap's BaZi Structures series of books comprises 5 individual titles to help you interact with the world.

While your Day Master shows you who you are, your Structure tells you about your behaviour and attitude in relation to the world. In this series, your strengths and weaknesses in how you relate to people and events in terms of work, family, and friendship all come to the fore. Each book in this series concentrates on one specific Structure, and provides clues on ideal careers, job roles, and wealth paths for that Structure.

Furthermore, these 5 guides will provide the blueprint to knowing why some people are the way they are, and what to do to help you deal with the varied and colourful characters in your life.

Your BaZi Profile – The Roles You Play in Life

Joey Yap's BaZi Profiles series of books comprises 10 individual titles that will reveal your personal, social and work masks you naturally exhibit in life.

Each BaZi Profile reveals a person's self-image which shows how the individual considers themselves consciously and unconsciously. A person's self-image determines how he/she sees the world, and how they respond to it. How a person sees the world ultimately determines what makes them happy and what success means to them. Every individual is different. Learn to see the world through the lens of 10 different profiles! Each profile can be at different states ranging from healthy to unhealthy.

By learning about your BaZi Profile you become AWARE of your strengths and weaknesses and begin the process of positive CHANGE.

Awareness is the first step for change and positive life transformation. With awareness comes realization. With realization – we discover ourselves.

These 10 books will provide you with new insights to your life. Discover a whole new world of YOU.

Continue Your Journey with Joey Yap's Books

Walking the Dragons

Walking the Dragons is a guided tour through the classical landform Feng Shui of ancient China, an enchanting collection of deeply-researched yet entertaining essays rich in historical detail.

Compiled in one book for the first time from Joey Yap's Feng Shui Mastery Excursion Series, the book highlights China's extensive, vibrant history with astute observations on the Feng Shui of important sites and places. Learn the landform formations of Yin Houses (tombs and burial places), as well as mountains, temples, castles, and villages.

It demonstrates complex Feng Shui theories and principles in easy-to-understand, entertaining language and is the perfect addition to the bookshelf of a Feng Shui or history lover. Anyone, whether experienced in Feng Shui or new to the practice, will be able to enjoy the insights shared in this book. Complete with gorgeous full-colour pictures of all the amazing sights and scenery, it's the next best thing to having been there yourself!

Your Aquarium Here

Your Aquarium Here is a simple, practical, hands-on Feng Shui book that teaches you how to incorporate a Water feature – an aquarium – for optimal Feng Shui benefit, whether for personal relationships, wealth, or career. Designed to be comprehensive yet simple enough for a novice or beginner, *Your Aquarium Here* provides historical and factual information about the role of Water in Feng Shui, and provides a step-by-step guide to installing and using an aquarium.

The book is the first in the **Fengshuilogy Series**, a series of matter-of-fact and useful Feng Shui books designed for the person who wants to do fuss-free Feng Shui. Not everyone who wants to use Feng Shui is an expert or a scholar! This series of books are just the kind you'd want on your bookshelf to gain basic, practical knowledge of the subject. Go ahead and Feng Shui-It-Yourself – *Your Aquarium Here* eliminates all the fuss and bother, but maintains all the fun and excitement, of authentic Feng Shui application!

The Art of Date Selection: Personal Date Selection

In today's modern world, it is not good enough to just do things effectively – we need to do them efficiently, as well. From the signing of business contracts and moving into a new home, to launching a product or even tying the knot; everything has to move, and move very quickly too. There is a premium on Time, where mistakes can indeed be costly.

The notion of doing the Right Thing, at the Right Time and in the Right Place is the very backbone of Date Selection. Because by selecting a suitable date specially tailored to a specific activity or endeavor, we infuse it with the most positive energies prevalent in our environment during that particular point in time; and that could well make the difference between `make-and-break'! With the *Art of Date Selection: Personal Date Selection*, learn simple, practical methods you can employ to select not just good dates, but personalized good dates. Whether it's a personal activity such as a marriage or professional endeavor such as launching a business, signing a contract or even acquiring assets, this book will show you how to pick the good dates and tailor them to suit the activity in question, as well as avoid the negative ones too!

The Art of Date Selection: Feng Shui Date Selection

Date Selection is the Art of selecting the most suitable date, where the energies present on the day support the specific activities or endeavors we choose to undertake on that day. Feng Shui is the Chinese Metaphysical study of the Physiognomy of the Land – landforms and the Qi they produce, circulate and conduct. Hence, anything that exists on this Earth is invariably subject to the laws of Feng Shui. So what do we get when Date Selection and Feng Shui converge?

Feng Shui Date Selection, of course! Say you wish to renovate your home, or maybe buy or rent one. Or perhaps, you're a developer, and wish to know WHEN is the best date possible to commence construction works on your project. In any case – and all cases – you certainly wish to ensure that your endeavors are well supported by the positive energies present on a good day, won't you? And this is where Date Selection supplements the practice of Feng Shui. At the end of the day, it's all about making the most of what's good, and minimizing what's bad.

(Available Soon)

Continue Your Journey with Joey Yap's Books

Feng Shui For Homebuyers - Exterior (English & Chinese versions)

Best selling Author and international Feng Shui Consultant, Joey Yap, will guide you on the various important features in your external environment that have a bearing on the Feng Shui of your home. For homeowners, those looking to build their own home or even investors who are looking to apply Feng Shui to their homes, this book provides valuable information from the classical Feng Shui theories and applications.

This book will assist you in screening and eliminating unsuitable options with negative FSQ (Feng Shui Quotient) should you acquire your own land or if you are purchasing a newly built home. It will also help you in determining which plot of land to select and which to avoid when purchasing an empty parcel of land.

Feng Shui for Homebuyers - Interior (English & Chinese versions)

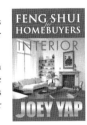

A book every homeowner or potential house buyer should have. The Feng Shui for Homebuyers (Interior) is an informative reference book and invaluable guide written by best selling Author and international Feng Shui Consultant, Joey Yap.

This book provides answers to the important questions of what really does matter when looking at the internal Feng Shui of a home or office. It teaches you how to analyze your home or office floor plans and how to improve their Feng Shui. It will answer all your questions about the positive and negative flow of Qi within your home and ways to utilize them to your maximum benefit.

Providing you with a guide to calculating your Life Gua and House Gua to fine-tune your Feng Shui within your property, Joey Yap focuses on practical, easily applicable ideas on what you can implement internally in a property.

Feng Shui for Apartment Buyers - Home Owners

Finding a good apartment or condominium is never an easy task but who do you ensure that is also has good Feng Shui? And how exactly do you apply Feng Shui to an apartment or condominium or high-rise residence?

These questions and more are answered by renowned Feng Shui Consultant and Master Trainer Joey Yap in **Feng Shui for Apartment Buyers - Home Owners**. Joey answers the key questions about Feng Shui and apartments, then guides you through the bare basics like taking a direction and super-imposing a Flying Stars chart onto a floor plan. Joey also walks you through the process of finding an apartment with favorable Feng Shui, sharing with you some of the key methods and techniques that are employed by professional Feng Shui consultants in assesing apartment Feng Shui.

In his trademark straight-to-the-point manner, Joey shares with you the Feng Shui do's and dont's when it comes to finding an apartment with favorable Feng Shui and which is conducive for home living.

The Ten Thousand Year Calendar

The Ten Thousand Year Calendar or 萬年曆 Wan Nian Li is a regular reference book and an invaluable tool used by masters, practitioners and students of Feng Shui, BaZi (Four Pillars of Destiny), Chinese Zi Wei Dou Shu Astrology (Purple Star), Yi Jing (I-Ching) and Date Selection specialists.

JOEY YAP's *Ten Thousand Year Calendar* provides the Gregorian (Western) dates converted into both the Chinese Solar and Lunar calendar in both the English and Chinese language.

It also includes a comprehensive set of key Feng Shui and Chinese Astrology charts and references, including Xuan Kong Nine Palace Flying Star Charts, Monthly and Daily Flying Stars, Water Dragon Formulas Reference Charts, Zi Wei Dou Shu (Purple Star) Astrology Reference Charts, BaZi (Four Pillars of Destiny) Heavenly Stems, Earthly Branches and all other related reference tables for Chinese Metaphysical Studies.

Continue Your Journey with Joey Yap's Books

Stories and Lessons on Feng Shui (English & Chinese versions)

Stories and Lessons on Feng Shui is a compilation of essays and stories written by leading Feng Shui and Chinese Astrology trainer and consultant Joey Yap about Feng Shui and Chinese Astrology.

In this heart-warming collection of easy to read stories, find out why it's a myth that you should never have Water on the right hand side of your house, the truth behind the infamous 'love' and 'wealth' corners and that the sudden death of a pet fish is really NOT due to bad luck!

More Stories and Lessons on Feng Shui

Finally, the long-awaited sequel to *Stories & Lessons on Feng Shui*!

If you've read the best-selling Stories & Lessons on Feng Shui, you won't want to miss this book. And even if you haven't read *Stories & Lessons on Feng Shui*, there's always a time to rev your Feng Shui engine up.

The time is NOW.

And the book? *More Stories & Lessons on Feng Shui* – the 2nd compilation of the most popular articles and columns penned by Joey Yap; **specially featured in national and international publications, magazines and newspapers.**

All in all, *More Stories & Lessons on Feng Shui* is a delightful chronicle of Joey's articles, thoughts and vast experience - as a professional Feng Shui consultant and instructor - that have been purposely refined, edited and expanded upon to make for a light-hearted, interesting yet educational read. And with Feng Shui, BaZi, Mian Xiang and Yi Jing all thrown into this one dish, there's something for everyone...so all you need to serve or accompany *More Stories & Lessons on Feng Shui* with is your favorite cup of tea or coffee!

Even More Stories and Lessons on Feng Shui

In this third release in the Stories and Lessons series, Joey Yap continues his exploration on the study and practice of Feng Shui in the modern age through a series of essays and personal anecdotes. Debunking superstition, offering simple and understandable "Feng Shui-It-Yourself" tips, and expounding on the history and origins of classical Feng Shui, Joey takes readers on a journey that is always refreshing and exciting.

Besides 'behind-the-scenes' revelations of actual Feng Shui audits, there are also chapters on how beginners can easily and accurately incorporate Feng Shui practice into their lives, as well as travel articles that offer proof that when it comes to Feng Shui, the Qi literally knows no boundaries.

In his trademark lucid and forthright style, Joey covers themes and topics that will strike a chord with all readers who have an interest in Feng Shui.

Mian Xiang - Discover Face Reading (English & Chinese versions)

Need to identify a suitable business partner? How about understanding your staff or superiors better? Or even choosing a suitable spouse? These mind boggling questions can be answered in Joey Yap's introductory book to Face Reading titled *Mian Xiang – Discover Face Reading*. This book will help you discover the hidden secrets in a person's face.

Mian Xiang – Discover Face Reading is comprehensive book on all areas of Face Reading, covering some of the most important facial features, including the forehead, mouth, ears and even the philtrum above your lips. This book will help you analyse not just your Destiny but help you achieve your full potential and achieve life fulfillment.

Continue Your Journey with Joey Yap's Books

BaZi - The Destiny Code (English & Chinese versions)

Leading Chinese Astrology Master Trainer Joey Yap makes it easy to learn how to unlock your Destiny through your BaZi with this book. BaZi or Four Pillars of Destiny is an ancient Chinese science which enables individuals to understand their personality, hidden talents and abilities as well as their luck cycle, simply by examining the information contained within their birth data. The Destiny Code is the first book that shows readers how to plot and interpret their own Destiny charts and lays the foundation for more in-depth BaZi studies. Written in a lively entertaining style, the Destiny Code makes BaZi accessible to the layperson. Within 10 chapters, understand and appreciate more about this astoundingly accurate ancient Chinese Metaphysical science.

BaZi - The Destiny Code Revealed

In this follow up to Joey Yap's best-selling The Destiny Code, delve deeper into your own Destiny chart through an understanding of the key elemental relationships that affect the Heavenly Stems and Earthly Branches. Find out how Combinations, Clash, Harm, Destructions and Punishments bring new dimension to a BaZi chart. Complemented by extensive real-life examples, The Destiny Code Revealed takes you to the next level of BaZi, showing you how to unlock the Codes of Destiny and to take decisive action at the right time, and capitalise on the opportunities in life.

Xuan Kong: Flying Stars Feng Shui

Xuan Kong Flying Stars Feng Shui is an essential introductory book to the subject of Xuan Kong Fei Xing, a well-known and popular system of Feng Shui, written by International Feng Shui Master Trainer Joey Yap.

In his down-to-earth, entertaining and easy to read style, Joey Yap takes you through the essential basics of Classical Feng Shui, and the key concepts of Xuan Kong Fei Xing (Flying Stars). Learn how to fly the stars, plot a Flying Star chart for your home or office and interpret the stars and star combinations. Find out how to utilise the favourable areas of your home or office for maximum benefit and learn 'tricks of the trade' and 'trade secrets' used by Feng Shui practitioners to enhance and maximise Qi in your home or office.

An essential integral introduction to the subject of Classical Feng Shui and the Flying Stars System of Feng Shui!

Xuan Kong Flying Stars: Structures and Combinations

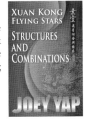

Delve deeper into Flying Stars through a greater understanding of the 81 Combinations and the influence of the Annual and Monthly Stars on the Base, Sitting and Facing Stars in this 2nd book in the Xuan Kong Feng Shui series. Learn how Structures like the Combination of 10, Up the Mountain and Down the River, Pearl and Parent String Structures are used to interpret a Flying Star chart.

(Available Soon)

Xuan Kong Flying Stars: Advanced Techniques

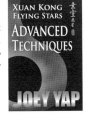

Take your knowledge of Xuan Kong Flying Stars to a higher level and learn how to apply complex techniques and advanced formulas such as Castle Gate Technique, Seven Star Robbery Formation, Advancing the Dragon Formation and Replacement Star technique amongst others. Joey Yap also shows you how to use the Life Palace technique to combine Gua Numbers with Flying Star Numbers and utilise the predictive facets of Flying Stars Feng Shui.

(Available Soon)

Elevate Your Feng Shui Skills With Joey Yap's Home Study Course And Educational DVDs

Xuan Kong Vol.1
An Advanced Feng Shui Home Study Course

Learn the Xuan Kong Flying Star Feng Shui system in just 20 lessons! Joey Yap's specialised notes and course work have been written to enable distance learning without compromising on the breadth or quality of the syllabus. Learn at your own pace with the same material students in a live class would use. The most comprehensive distance learning course on Xuan Kong Flying Star Feng Shui in the market. Xuan Kong Flying Star Vol.1 comes complete with a special binder for all your course notes.

Feng Shui for Period 8 - (DVD)

Don't miss the Feng Shui Event of the next 20 years! Catch Joey Yap LIVE and find out just what Period 8 is all about. This DVD boxed set zips you through the fundamentals of Feng Shui and the impact of this important change in the Feng Shui calendar. Joey's entertaining, conversational style walks you through the key changes that Period 8 will bring and how to tap into Wealth Qi and Good Feng Shui for the next 20 years.

Xuan Kong Flying Stars Beginners Workshop - (DVD)

Take a front row seat in Joey Yap's Xuan Kong Flying Stars workshop with this unique LIVE RECORDING of Joey Yap's Xuan Kong Flying Stars Feng Shui workshop, attended by over 500 people. This DVD program provides an effective and quick introduction of Xuan Kong Feng Shui essentials for those who are just starting out in their study of classical Feng Shui. Learn to plot your own Flying Star chart in just 3 hours. Learn 'trade secret' methods, remedies and cures for Flying Stars Feng Shui. This boxed set contains 3 DVDs and 1 workbook with notes and charts for reference.

BaZi Four Pillars of Destiny Beginners Workshop - (DVD)

Ever wondered what Destiny has in store for you? Or curious to know how you can learn more about your personality and inner talents? BaZi or Four Pillars of Destiny is an ancient Chinese science that enables us to understand a person's hidden talent, inner potential, personality, health and wealth luck from just their birth data. This specially compiled DVD set of Joey Yap's BaZi Beginners Workshop provides a thorough and comprehensive introduction to BaZi. Learn how to read your own chart and understand your own luck cycle. This boxed set contains 3 DVDs and 1 workbook with notes and reference charts.

Interested in learning MORE about Feng Shui? Advance Your Feng Shui Knowledge with the Mastery Academy Courses.

Feng Shui Mastery Series™
LIVE COURSES (MODULES ONE TO FOUR)

Feng Shui Mastery – Module One
Beginners Course

Designed for students seeking an entry-level intensive program into the study of Feng Shui , Module One is an intensive foundation course that aims not only to provide you with an introduction to Feng Shui theories and formulas and equip you with the skills and judgments to begin practicing and conduct simple Feng Shui audits upon successful completion of the course. Learn all about Forms, Eight Mansions Feng Shui and Flying Star Feng Shui in just one day with a unique, structured learning program that makes learning Feng Shui quick and easy!

Feng Shui Mastery – Module Two
Practitioners Course

Building on the knowledge and foundation in classical Feng Shui theory garnered in M1, M2 provides a more advanced and in-depth understanding of Eight Mansions, Xuan Kong Flying Star and San He and introduces students to theories that are found only in the classical Chinese Feng Shui texts. This 3-Day Intensive course hones analytical and judgment skills, refines Luo Pan (Chinese Feng Shui compass) skills and reveals 'trade secret' remedies. Module Two covers advanced Forms Analysis, San He's Five Ghost Carry Treasure formula, Advanced Eight Mansions and Xuan Kong Flying Stars and equips you with the skills needed to undertake audits and consultations for residences and offices.

Feng Shui Mastery – Module Three
Advanced Practitioners Course

Module Three is designed for Professional Feng Shui Practitioners. Learn advanced topics in Feng Shui and take your skills to a cutting edge level. Be equipped with the knowledge, techniques and confidence to conduct large scale audits (like estate and resort planning). Learn how to apply different systems appropriately to remedy situations or cases deemed inauspicious by one system and reconcile conflicts in different systems of Feng Shui. Gain advanced knowledge of San He (Three Harmony) systems and San Yuan (Three Cycles) systems, advanced Luan Tou (Forms Feng Shui) and specialist Water Formulas.

Feng Shui Mastery – Module Four
Master Course

The graduating course of the Feng Shui Mastery (FSM) Series, this course takes the advanced practitioner to the Master level. Power packed M4 trains students to 'walk the mountains' and identify superior landform, superior grade structures and make qualitative evaluations of landform, structures, Water and Qi and covers advanced and exclusive topics of San He, San Yuan, Xuan Kong, Ba Zhai, Luan Tou (Advanced Forms and Water Formula) Feng Shui. Master Internal, External and Luan Tou (Landform) Feng Shui methodologies to apply Feng Shui at every level and undertake consultations of every scale and magnitude, from houses and apartments to housing estates, townships, shopping malls and commercial districts.

BaZi Mastery Series™
LIVE COURSES (MODULES ONE TO FOUR)

BaZi Mastery – Module One
Intensive Foundation Course

This Intensive One Day Foundation Course provides an introduction to the principles and fundamentals of BaZi (Four Pillars of Destiny) and Destiny Analysis methods such as Ten Gods, Useful God and Strength of Qi. Learn how to plot a BaZi chart and interpret your Destiny and your potential. Master BaZi and learn to capitalize on your strengths, minimize risks and downturns and take charge of your Destiny.

BaZi Mastery – Module Two
Practitioners Course

BaZi Module Two teaches students advanced BaZi analysis techniques and specific analysis methods for relationship luck, health evaluation, wealth potential and career potential. Students will learn to identify BaZi chart structures, sophisticated methods for applying the Ten Gods, and how to read Auxiliary Stars. Students who have completed Module Two will be able to conduct professional BaZi readings.

BaZi Mastery – Module Three
Advanced Practitioners Course

Designed for the BaZi practitioner, learn how to read complex cases and unique events in BaZi charts and perform Big and Small assessments. Discover how to analyze personalities and evaluate talents precisely, as well as special formulas and classical methodologies for BaZi from classics such as Di Tian Sui and Qiong Tong Bao Jian.

BaZi Mastery – Module Four
Master Course in BaZi

The graduating course of the BaZi Mastery Series, this course takes the advanced practitioner to the Masters' level. BaZi M4 focuses on specialized techniques of BaZi reading, unique special structures and advance methods from ancient classical texts. This program includes techniques on date selection and ancient methodologies from the Qiong Tong Bao Jian and Yuan Hai Zi Ping classics.

Xuan Kong Mastery – Module One
Advanced Foundation Course

This course is for the experienced Feng Shui professionals who wish to expand their knowledge and skills in the Xuan Kong system of Feng Shui, covering important foundation methods and techniques from the Wu Chang and Guang Dong lineages of Xuan Kong Feng Shui.

Xuan Kong Mastery – Module Two A
Advanced Xuan Kong Methodologies

Designed for Feng Shui practitioners seeking to specialise in the Xuan Kong system, this program focuses on methods of application and Joey Yap's unique Life Palace and Shifting Palace Methods, as well as methods and techniques from the Wu Chang lineage.

Xuan Kong Mastery – Module Two B
Purple White

Explore in detail and in great depth the star combinations in Xuan Kong. Learn how each different combination reacts or responds in different palaces, under different environmental circumstances and to whom in the property. Learn methods, theories and techniques extracted from ancient classics such as Xuan Kong Mi Zhi, Xuan Kong Fu, Fei Xing Fu and Zi Bai Jue.

Xuan Kong Mastery – Module Three
Advanced Xuan Kong Da Gua

This intensive course focuses solely on the Xuan Kong Da Gua system covering the theories, techniques and methods of application of this unique 64-Hexagram based system of Xuan Kong including Xuan Kong Da Gua for landform analysis.

Walk the Mountains! Learn Feng Shui in a Practical and Hands-on Program

Feng Shui Mastery Excursion Series™ : CHINA

Learn landform (Luan Tou) Feng Shui by walking the mountains and chasing the Dragon's vein in China. This Program takes the students in a study tour to examine notable Feng Shui landmarks, mountains, hills, valleys, ancient palaces, famous mansions, houses and tombs in China. The Excursion is a 'practical' hands-on course where students are shown to perform readings using the formulas they've learnt and to recognize and read Feng Shui Landform (Luan Tou) formations.

Read about China Excursion here:
http://www.masteryacademy.com/Education/schoolfengshui/fengshuimasteryexcursion.asp

Mian Xiang Mastery Series™
LIVE COURSES (MODULES ONE AND TWO)

Mian Xiang Mastery – Module One
Basic Face Reading

A person's face is their fortune – learn more about the ancient Chinese art of Face Reading. In just one day, be equipped with techniques and skills to read a person's face and ascertain their character, luck, wealth and relationship luck.

Mian Xiang Mastery – Module Two
Practical Face Reading

Mian Xiang Module Two covers face reading techniques extracted from the ancient classics Shen Xiang Quan Pian and Shen Xiang Tie Guan Dau. Gain a greater depth and understanding of Mian Xiang and learn to recognize key structures and characteristics in a person's face.

Yi Jing Mastery Series™
LIVE COURSES (MODULES ONE AND TWO)

Yi Jing Mastery – Module One
Traditional Yi Jing

'Yi', relates to change. Change is the only constant in life and the universe, without exception to this rule. The Yi Jing is hence popularly referred to as the Book or Classic of Change. Discoursed in the language of Yin and Yang, the Yi Jing is one of the oldest Chinese classical texts surviving today. With Traditional Yi Jing, learnn how this Classic is used to divine the outcomes of virtually every facet of life; from your relationships to seeking an answer to the issues you may face in your daily life.

Yi Jing Mastery – Module Two
Plum Blossom Numerology

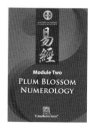

Shao Yong, widely regarded as one of the greatest scholars of the Sung Dynasty, developed Mei Hua Yi Shu (Plum Blossom Numerology) as a more advanced means for divination purpose using the Yi Jing. In Plum Blossom Numerology, the results of a hexagram are interpreted by referring to the Gua meanings, where the interaction and relationship between the five elements, stems, branches and time are equally taken into consideration. This divination method, properly applied, allows us to make proper decisions whenever we find ourselves in a predicament.

Ze Ri Mastery Series™
LIVE COURSES (MODULES ONE AND TWO)

Ze Ri Mastery Series Module 1
Personal and Feng Shui Date Selection

The Mastery Academy's Date Selection Mastery Series Module 1 is specifically structured to provide novice students with an exciting introduction to the Art of Date Selection. Learn the rudiments and tenets of this intriguing metaphysical science. What makes a good date, and what makes a bad date? What dates are suitable for which activities, and what dates simply aren't? And of course, the mother of all questions: WHY aren't all dates created equal. All in only one Module – Module 1!

Ze Ri Mastery Series Module 2
Xuan Kong Da Gua Date Selection

In Module 2, discover advanced Date Selection techniques that will take your knowledge of this Art to a level equivalent to that of a professional's! This is the Module where Date Selection infuses knowledge of the ancient metaphysical science of Feng Shui and BaZi (Chinese Astrology, or Four Pillars of Destiny). Feng Shui, as a means of maximizing Human Luck (i.e. our luck on Earth), is often quoted as the cure to BaZi, which allows us to decipher our Heaven (i.e. inherent) Luck. And one of the most potent ways of making the most of what life has to offer us is to understand our Destiny, know how we can use the natural energies of our environment for our environments and MOST importantly, WHEN we should use these energies and for WHAT endeavors!

You will learn specific methods on how to select suitable dates, tailored to specific activities and events. More importantly, you will also be taught how to suit dates to a person's BaZi (Chinese Astrology, or Four Pillars of Destiny), in order to maximize his or her strengths, and allow this person to surmount any challenges that lie in wait. Add in the factor of 'place', and you would have satisfied the notion of 'doing the right thing, at the right time and in the right place'! A basic knowledge of BaZi and Feng Shui will come in handy in this Module, although these are not pre-requisites to successfully undergo Module 2.

Feng Shui for Life

Feng Shui for life is a 5-day course designed for the Feng Shui beginner to learn how to apply practical Feng Shui in day-to-day living. It is a culmination of powerful tools and techniques that allows you to gain quick proficiency in Classical Feng Shui. Discover quick tips on analysing your own BaZi, how to apply Feng Shui solutions for your own home, how to select auspicious dates for important activities, as well as simple and useful Face Reading techniques and practical Water Formulas. This is a complete beginner's course that is suitable for anyone with an interest in applying practical, real-world Feng Shui for life! Enhance every aspect of your life – your health, wealth, and relationships – using these easy-to-apply Classical Feng Shui methods.

Mastery Academy courses are conducted around the world. Find out when will Joey Yap be in your area by visiting **www.masteryacademy.com** or call our office at **+603-2284 8080**.